MAKE TIME FOR
CLOCKS

30
UNIQUE
DESIGNS
for Your Home

COMPILED BY CHRIS WALLACE

Published by

kp **krause publications**
An F&W Publications Company

700 East State Street • Iola, WI 54990-0001
715-445-2214 • 888-457-2873
www.krause.com

Please call or write for our free catalog of publications. To place an order or obtain a free catalog, please call 800-258-0929. Please use our regular business telephone 715-445-2214 for editorial comment or further information.

Library of Congress Catalog Number 2002113131
ISBN 0-87349-637-X

Contents

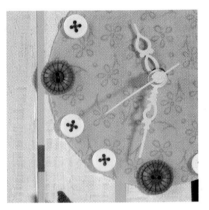

It's Time to
Make Clocks

*Time flies, take time to smell the flowers,
don't let time pass you by, I don't have enough time,
it's time to go, it's about time that happened.*

Well, you get the point. Everyone has time, needs time, and wants more of it. And now it's time to make clocks!

We know the time of day by looking at a clock, so it makes sense to create clocks for each room of our living spaces. In this book there's a great mix of projects for any skill level from beginner to advanced. You'll find many new ideas using innovative techniques by some of the most respected and talented designers and artists.

A clock can be made out of anything that can have a hole drilled into it. It can be made from an item you already have, a yard sale find, or something you purchase from a craft store. The clock faces, movements, hands, and numbers also can be found in craft stores, and the instructions for attaching any clock piece to any type of surface is shown very clearly on the back of the packaging. With so many different types of surfaces, movements, hands, faces, numbers and bezels, you are sure to find something that is just right for you.

Working with all of these wonderful designers was truly a joy. When the clocks began to arrive to be photographed, it was just like Christmas. Of course, the best part is being able to share them with you.

Special thanks to Hansen's TV Appliances & Home Furnishings of Waupaca, Wisconsin, who graciously allowed us the use of their store for photography purposes.

Basic Information and Definitions of Terms

Wood and Moisture Content

The pine and basswood products used throughout this book were kiln dried to a 6-8% moisture content. It is important to use wood products that have only 6-8% moisture content so the wood will not crack or warp in a home environment. The time spent creating these timepieces is valuable, and the pieces created will become heirlooms for future generations.

Preparing and Sealing Wood Surfaces

During the manufacturing process, nails are sometimes used. The process leaves a hole that needs to be filled with putty. After filling holes, let dry, then sand lightly to smooth the surface. The wood product is now ready for sealing.

Some projects use techniques that might require sealing the wood after a beginning step, such as woodburning. Some projects use painting techniques in which the designer wants to paint directly on the raw wood due to better results obtained for a particular technique. Unless otherwise directed, most wood surfaces should be prepared with a wood sealer before painting. Some wood sealers penetrate the wood, while others sit on top of the wood. One coat of wood sealer is all that is needed to seal the wood. Regardless of which type is used, it will be necessary to lightly sand with fine grade sandpaper after the wood sealer is dry. Always sand in the direction of the grain of the wood.

Batteries Needed

All clock movements will need a battery to function. Check package for battery size.

Glossary of Terms

Basecoat

To give an opaque coating to a surface, use a large, flat brush or sponge brush to smoothly apply a coat of paint. If a second coat is needed, always let the paint dry completely between coats.

Comma Stroke (Round Brush)

With bristles fully loaded, press bristles onto surface so that the end of brush rounds out. Slowly begin pulling the stroke and release pressure, letting bristles return to original shape, lift off surface.

Dots

Dip stylus, toothpick, or wooden end of brush into fresh paint and touch surface to create dot. For descending dots, load only once. For dots that are uniform size, dip tool into paint after each dot.

Double Load

With a different color of paint on each half of a slightly damp flat brush, stroke over and over in the same place on palette until the two colors merge in the brush center, creating a blend.

Dry Brush

Dip brush into paint. Wipe off almost all of paint onto paper towel. Brush over surface with little or no pressure. Color may be intensified by dry brushing over the same area, letting each coat of paint dry between applications.

Floating Color

Dip a flat brush in water and remove excess water by blotting on a paper towel. Pick up paint on one corner of the brush and blend back and forth on palette in one spot until color moves gradually across bristle to clear water on opposite side of brush.

Spatter

This application is generally applied after other techniques are completed. Add water to paint for a thin consistency. Dip an old toothbrush into paint and carefully use finger to pull bristles away from surface, so that spatters of paint drop onto the desired area.

Wash

To create a transparent look, thin paint with water. To achieve a smooth application, use a large brush to apply paint to surface.

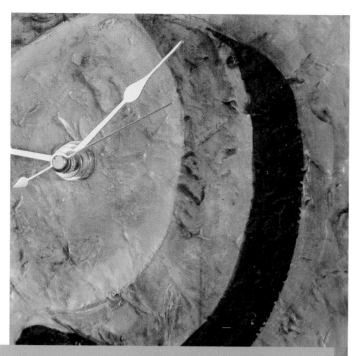

PRISCILLA HAUSER
STRAW HAT

FINISHED SIZE: 8" X 11"

This delightful technique easily creates the look of a straw hat using facial tissues, water-based varnish, and a little paint.

MATERIALS

Basswood Country Plank*
Clock movement and hands for ¾"
    surface*
Acrylic paint*:
    Turner's Yellow
    Burnt Umber
    Warm White
    Asphaltum
    Pure Black
Paint mediums:
    Glazing
    Blending gel
Brushes*: #10, 12, 14 shader, 1" wash
    brush, 1" sponge brush

100% cotton rags or piece of old
    T-shirt, brush basin, facial tissues,
    fine sandpaper, graphite paper,
    palette, palette knife, pencil, piece of
    plain brown paper bag, tack cloth,
    tracing paper, water-based varnish

* These products were used: Walnut
    Hollow® plank, clock movements •
    Folk Art® paints, mediums • Loew-
    Cornell® brushes

Note: *Refer to color photos for application and placement. Let paint and varnish dry between applications.*

INSTRUCTIONS

Please refer to Straw Hat pattern on page 108.

1. Sand clock with fine-grade sandpaper and wipe with tack cloth.
2. Mix stain on palette with palette knife using 2 parts Asphaltum and 5 parts of Glazing Medium. Use 1" sponge brush to apply two coats mixture to entire clock surface. Wipe excess with rag.
3. To smooth surface, rub with piece of plain brown paper bag.
4. Neatly trace hat design onto tracing paper with pencil. Transfer design by placing graphite paper between traced design and clock. Retrace lines with pencil to transfer outside edge of hat only.
5. Separate several facial tissues into individual layers, tearing into small pieces. To glue tissue to hat design, use sponge brush to apply generous amount of varnish to design. Place torn pieces of tissue all over design, allowing some pieces to overlap. Apply more varnish over tissue.
6. Use pencil and graphite paper to transfer inner hat design and bow onto dried tissue.
7. To shade under right side of hat design, double load 1" wash brush with Glazing Medium on one side and Burnt Umber on other. Pat and blend to soften color.
8. To shade and highlight each section of hat, apply a small amount of Blending Gel Medium, working each section separately. Add more Blending Gel Medium as needed.
9. To paint brim, use #14 shader to apply Turner's Yellow. Shade with Asphaltum, highlight with Warm White.
10. To paint very top of hat, use #12 shader to apply Turner's Yellow. Shade with Asphaltum, highlight with Warm White.
11. To paint side of top, use #10 shader to apply Turner's Yellow. Shade with Asphaltum.
12. To paint ribbon, use #10 to apply Pure Black. Highlight with Warm White.
13. To varnish, use 1" wash brush to apply 2-3 coats of water-based varnish to entire clock surface.
14. Attach clock movement and hands following directions on back of packaging.

straw hat

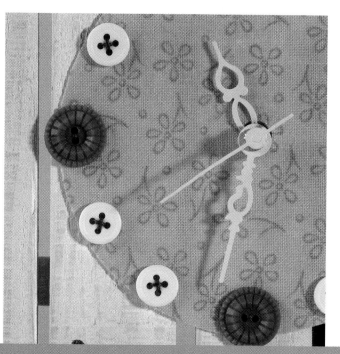

Wooden picket fence*
Clock movement for ⅜" surface*
1⅜" clock hands*
Assorted bright fabric scraps including
    light, medium, and dark green
Sewing thread to match flower fabrics
    plus dark green
Two ¾" wood split snowmen
    (ladybugs)
Buttons: Thirteen assorted ⅜"-1¹¹⁄₁₆"
    white (flower centers)
    Eight ⅜" white (clock face)
    Four ⅝" green (clock face)
4" square iron-on backing
48" 18-gauge Plastic Fun Wire*:
    Sour Apple
Acrylic paint:
    White
    Red
    Black
White spray paint
Spray matte varnish
Two small screw eyes
Wire, fish line, or ribbon for hanger
Fabric glue*

Compass, drill with ⅜" bit, hand sewing
    needle, iron, large and small brushes,
    palette, pencil, rags, ruler, scissors,
    toothpick

* These products were used: Walnut
    Hollow® picket fence, clock
    movement, clock hands • Toner™
    wire • Beacon® glue

Note: *Refer to color photos for
applications and placement. Let paint,
varnish, and glue dry between
applications.*

CHRIS MALONE
ENGLISH COTTAGE

FINISHED SIZE: 10½" X 8¼" X ¾"

*This flowered picket fence is a whimsical suggestion
of an English cottage garden. Scattered fabric leaves
and yo-yo flowers add bright colors to the garden.
Let the button markings help you tell time.*

INSTRUCTIONS

Please refer to English Cottage pattern on page 106.

1. Thin White paint with water, use large brush
   to apply on fence and immediately rub off
   excess with rag to produce white-washed
   effect. Spray with two light coats of matte
   varnish.

2. To make lady bugs, use small brush to paint
   body of split snowman red and head black.
   Use tip of toothpick to make white dots for
   eyes and six black dots on back. Paint a
   wiggly black line down center of back. Spray
   with matte varnish.

3. To make yo-yo flowers, use compass to make
   patterns and cut circles from assorted fabrics:
   3 (4"), 3 (3½"), 4 (3"), and 3 (2½"). For each
   flower, finger press a ⅛" hem, sew gathering
   stitch all around edge, near fold, with
   matching thread (doubled). Pull thread to
   gather edges into a tight circle; flatten flower
   with fingers so hole is in center of flower.
   Knot thread, sew button to flower center.

4. To make leaves, fold medium green and dark
   green fabric in half, right sides facing. Trace

around leaf patterns on one side of fabric,
making a total of six small and five large
leaves. Sew on traced lines, leaving open at
bottom. Cut out close to seam; turn right
side out. Fold small pleat at bottom; tack to
secure.

5. Follow manufacturer's directions to iron
   backing to wrong side of light green fabric.
   For clock face, cut a 3¾" circle. Use matching
   thread to sew a green button to 12, 3, 6, and
   9 positions on face, with button extending
   beyond edge of circle about ⅛". Evenly space
   white buttons around edge for remaining
   numbers; sew in place with green thread.

6. Spray paint clock hands White.

7. Drill hole with ⅜" bit for clock movement
   approximately 5⅛" above bottom of fence in
   center of one of tallest planks, checking that
   clock movement will clear horizontal slat on
   back of fence. Cut hole in center of clock face
   large enough for shank of clock. Glue face to
   fence, matching holes. Attach clock

english cottage

movement and hands following directions on back of packaging.

8. Arrange flowers, with leaves tucked under outer edges, on fence as desired. When satisfied with placement, glue to fence, applying glue to back of flower centers and inner edge of leaves only. Glue ladybugs to fence.

9. For tendrils, cut wire into five pieces, 8"-12" long. Bend into large circles. Apply glue to straight end of each piece and tuck under flower or leaf edge.

10. To hang clock, insert screw eyes into top of horizontal slat on back, one at each end.

11. Tie wire, fish line, or ribbon around screw eyes to make a hanger. Wire or fish line should be short enough to be covered by fence. Ribbon may be cut longer to hang above top of fence as decoration.

english cottage

Creative Woodburner*
Mini Flow Point*
Basswood teapot*
Clock movement for ¼" surface*
Gold clock hands*
Gold Arabic numerals*
Oil color pencils*:
  Alizarin Crimson
  Burnt Umber
  Celadon Green
  Olive Green
  Periwinkle
  Pink Rose
Satin interior spray varnish*
Acrylic paint*:
  Hydrangea Pink
  Village Green
  Wedgwood Green
  White
Stencil*: Vine frames and accents

¼" and ½" flat brushes, ½" masking tape, No. 2 pencil, drill with ⅜" bit, fine sandpaper, foam plate, graphite paper, heat-resistant surface (such as cookie sheet), needle-nose pliers, paper towels, scrap of wood for practice, sea sponge, soft large brush, small paper cup, tack cloth

* These products were used: Walnut Hollow® woodburner and point, teapot, clock movement, hands, numerals, oil pencils • Delta® paint, varnish, stencil

Note: Refer to color photos for application and placement. Let paint, varnish, and glue dry between applications.

VICKI SCHREINER
TIME FOR TEA

FINISHED SIZE: 6¾" X 7¼" X 4¼"

What a delightful way to know when it's time for tea. Create this clock with easy beginner woodburning techniques and add color with oil pencils.

INSTRUCTIONS

1. To prepare the teapot, lightly sand, wipe with tack cloth. Use small paper cup to mix equal parts White with water. Work on one side of teapot at a time. Use ½" brush to apply mixture, wiping off immediately with paper towel.

2. Use ½" brush to basecoat four knob feet, knob on lid, and outside edge of lid with Wedgwood Green.

3. Use masking tape on following areas on teapot to protect them from sponging step: around base of spout; around base of handle; all the way around bottom area of teapot above tapered edge. Work on spout, handle and bottom area of teapot as follows: Wet sea sponge with water until soft. Wring water out of sponge with paper towels until sponge is only damp. Place Village Green on foam plate, dab sponge into paint. Dab sponge once or twice on palette to remove some paint. Dab sponge onto surface, turning your wrist back and forth as you work to create a textured appearance. Sponge these same areas a second time using Hydrangea Pink.

4. Use No. 2 pencil to trace stencil design as follows: Trace corner design from frame stencil to top left and bottom right corners (above tapered edge) on front and back of teapot. Trace corner design to bottom left and bottom right corners (above tapered edge) on sides of teapot. Trace corner design to two opposite corners on lid.
   Note: Carefully follow manufacturer's safety instructions on package when using the wood-burning tool.

5. Before plugging in woodburning tool, remove universal point and replace with mini flow point, tighten with needle-nose pliers. Tape wire holder onto heat-resistant surface with masking tape. Place woodburning tool on holder, plug in, and allow to heat.

Note: *Practice a few strokes on a piece of scrap wood before working on project. Use slow, small sketching strokes instead of long continuous strokes. Do not use heavy pressure. The length of time you keep the tip on the surface of the wood determines the darkness, not pressure. Let the heat do the work. To maintain even heat flow, keep the tip clean by frequently dragging it across fine sandpaper. Relax and have fun!*

6. Woodburn outline of all traced stencil designs on teapot and lid. Add a vein line to each leaf, attaching it to stem. Apply several random scattered dots throughout designs as desired. Unplug woodburner tool.
Note: *When coloring, brush all pencil crumbs away using a large soft brush.*

7. To add color use oil color pencils as follows: Using medium pressure, color all flower petals Pink Rose, all leaves Celadon Green. Using medium pressure, add shading to inside area of each flower petal with Alizarin Crimson. Add shading to base of each leaf at stem with Olive Green. Use heavy pressure to blend shading by coloring designs once again with original color: All flower petals Pink Rose, all leaves Celadon Green. Darkly color centers of each flower and each small circle Periwinkle.

8. After all coloring is completed, clean out woodburned grooves by going along inside of each groove with Burnt Umber oil color pencil.

9. To set the oil colors, apply one light coat of spray varnish to entire teapot and lid. Apply one more coat of varnish.

10. Use numeral placement pattern with graphite paper to apply markings as follows: Lay pattern onto front of teapot and secure with two small pieces of masking tape. Slide graphite paper under pattern (graphite side down). Using the No. 2 pencil, trace the center dot, center circle, and number placement dots. Remove pattern.

11. Use drill with ⅜" bit to create hole for clock movement.

12. Adhere numerals in place. Attach clock movement and hands following directions on back of packaging.

time for tea

MATERIALS

Mini crate*
Medium sunburst adhesive clock face*
Clock movement with hands for ¼"
  surface*
4 toy wheels*
Four 1¼" ball knobs*
Acrylic paint*: Blue Danube, Lilac
All-purpose sealer*
Satin spray varnish*
Brushes*: ½" flat, #1 liner
4" x 5¾" matte board

Craft glue, drill with ⅜" bit, fine
  sandpaper, old toothbrush, paper
  towels, scissors, tack cloth, water
  container.

  *These products were used: Walnut
  Hollow® crate, clock face, clock
  movement, toy wheels, ball knobs •
  Delta® paint, sealer, varnish • Loew-
  Cornell® brushes

Note: *Refer to color photos for
application and placement. Let paint,
varnish, and glue dry between
applications.*

PAMELA HAWKINS
MINI CRATE
CLOCK PLANTER

FINISHED SIZE: 5¼" X 4" X 6½"

This nifty storage solution is a time keeper, too. Here's a way to make a clock that is a little more fun, yet functional. Let it come alive by tucking a plant inside—storage areas don't always have to hold papers and pens!

INSTRUCTIONS

1. Use ½" flat brush to apply one coat of sealer to crate. Sand lightly.
2. Use ½" flat brush to apply two coats Blue Danube to crate, matte board, and ball knobs.
3. Use ½" flat brush to apply two coats Lilac to wheels, inside crate handles, and top edge of crate.
4. Use craft glue to adhere matte board to inside of crate slats.
5. Use drill and ⅜" bit to create hole in center of middle slat for clock movement.
6. Use craft glue to attach wheels and ball knobs to crate.
7. Use #1 liner with Lilac to paint border line on crate.
8. For a spatter effect, thin Lilac with water (1:1). Use thinned Lilac on old toothbrush, pull finger across bristles to spatter entire crate.
9. For a protective finish, apply 2-3 coats of spray varnish.
10. Adhere clock face to crate.
11. Attach clock movement and hands following directions on back of packaging.

mini crate
clock planter

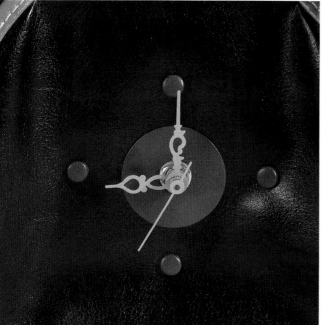

MATERIALS

Clock movement for ¼" surface*
Clock hands*
Three 1½" x ¹⁄₃₂" washers with ⅜"
   center
Four brass paper fasteners
Metal paint*: 2 colors to match purse
Purse

Brush, craft knife, rubbing alcohol,
   ruler, washable marker pen

*These products were used: Walnut
Hollow® clock movement, clock
hands • DecoArt™ metal paint

Note: *Refer to color photos for
application and placement. Let paint
dry between applications.*

KOREN RUSSELL
THE PURSE, THE CLOCK, AND THE PLANTER

FINISHED SIZE: 7" X 7" X 4"

The right purse can be hard to find, but once found, often hard to discard. With this project, you can keep the purse and give it a new stylish purpose—two, in fact.

INSTRUCTIONS

1. Wipe one washer and four brass fasteners with rubbing alcohol. Use brush to paint top and sides of washer and tops of fasteners with metal paint color of choice.
Note: If using a leather purse, paint last coat by pouncing and dabbing brush. This will create a texture similar to leather.

2. Use brush with second metal paint color of choice to paint clock hands.

3. On side of the purse planned for installing clock, find center point, mark with pen. Measure ½" directly above mark and place second mark. The second mark will be used. Wipe off first mark.

4. Use craft knife to cut a ⅜" x ⅜" "X" into purse on mark.

5. To attach clock movement and painted hands, follow directions on back of packaging. After pushing clock movement shaft into purse, carefully trim off excess purse material flaps from "X." Place painted washer over shaft. Add gold washer, hex nut, and hands.

6. Place marks at 12, 3, 6 and 9 o'clock positions, ⅝" from outer edge of washer.

7. Cut through purse at marks just long enough to fit paper fastener prongs. Insert one paper fastener into each cut, separate prongs, pushing against inside of purse.

the purse, the clock, and the planter

Flower clock/plaque*
Clock movement with hands for ¼"
   surface*
Circles*: 4 large (1⅛"), 8 medium (¾")
Dowels*: 4" length each of ³⁄₁₆" and ⅛"
   diameter
Spray paint*:
   Yellow
   Holiday Red
   Purple
   Orange
   Larkspur Blue
   Holiday Green
Clear finish sealer (matte)*
Acrylic paint*:
   Ebony Black
   Cool White
Wire*: 2 ft. length of 22 gauge Black
Thick craft glue*
Hot glue gun and glue sticks*
Size 1 script paint brush*

Craft snip, needle-nose pliers, ruler

* These products were used: Walnut
   Hollow® clock and clock movements
   • Forster® Woodsies® circles,
   dowels • Design Master® Color
   Tool® spray paint, sealer • DecoArt™
   Americana® acrylic paint • Artistic
   Wire • Aleene's® glue • Adhesive
   Tech™ hot glue gun and sticks •
   Loew-Cornell® brushes

Note: Refer to color photos for
application and placement. Let paint,
varnish, and glue dry between
applications.

CRAFT MARKETING CONNECTIONS
DON'T BUG ME

FINISHED SIZE: 9¼" ROUND

*This cute, whimsical clock is a great addition
to a child's room, family room, porch, or
patio. The brightly colored ladybugs seem to
be endlessly watching the hands of the clock
go around.*

INSTRUCTIONS

1. In a well-ventilated area, spray both wooden pieces of flower clock with Yellow. Varnish flower clock with matte sealer.

2. For ladybugs, spray large circles Holiday Red. Spray two medium circles in each of the following colors: Purple, Orange, Larkspur Blue, Holiday Green.
   Optional: Circles may be painted with acrylic paints.

3. For bug details, use script brush to paint head and center line with Ebony Black. Place dots on large circles with end of ³⁄₁₆" dowel dipped into Ebony Black. Place dots on small circles with ⅛" dowel. For eyes, use brush to make Cool White dots on bug heads.

4. To assemble large bugs, use a craft snip to cut 12 2"-pieces of wire for legs. Use needle-nose pliers to turn a loop at each end of all 12 wires. Gather three pieces of wire together and add a dot of hot glue to center of wires, binding them together. Repeat for remaining legs. Hot glue legs to bottom of large bug circles and separate legs.

5. Position and use craft glue to attach large bugs at 12, 3, 6, and 9 o'clock. Glue small bugs in place.

6. Attach clock movement and hands following directions on back of packaging.

7. Use craft glue to glue center piece of flower to flower clock.

don't bug me

MATERIALS

Large open based pendulum clock*
Large pendulum movement with
   hands*
Large pansies adhesive clock face*
Acrylic paint*:
   Black
   Village Green
   Mendocino Red
All-purpose sealer*
Satin spray varnish*
Brushes*: ¾" wash, #3 round

1" foam brush, paper plate, paper
   towels, fine sandpaper, tack cloth,
   water container

* These products were used: Walnut
   Hollow® clock, pendulum movement
   with hands, clock face • Delta®
   paint, sealer, varnish • Loew-Cornell®
   brushes

Note: *Refer to color photos for
application and placement. Let paint
and varnish dry between applications.*

CHRIS WALLACE
PANSY PENDULUM

FINISHED SIZE: 7½" X 19¼" X 4"

*This beautiful clock with a hand-painted look is easy to create. By using a clock face that is
an adhesive sticker, anyone can make it!*

1. To prepare clock, use sponge brush to apply
   one coat of sealer to entire clock. Use
   sandpaper to sand lightly, wipe with tack
   cloth.
2. To basecoat, use ¾" wash brush to apply
   Village Green and Mendocino Red. Use #3
   round to apply Black to routed edges.
3. Adhere adhesive clock face carefully. Press in
   place firmly with fingers. (See page 83.)
4. For a protective finish, spray entire clock
   with 2-3 coats of varnish.
5. Attach clock movement and hands following
   directions on back of packaging. Attach the
   pendulum to the clock movement.

pansy pendulum

MATERIALS

Small chair*
3-piece clock kit with numerals and
   hands for ⅜" surface*
Acrylic paint*:
   White
   Light Buttermilk
   Lemon Yellow
   Lavender
   Yellow Green
   Blush Flesh
Sealer/finisher satin varnish*
Six wooden beads
Brushes: #6 round, #4 flat, ¾" wash

Drill with ⅜" bit, fine sandpaper, sea
   sponge, tack cloth, wood filler, wood
   glue

*These products were used: Walnut
   Hollow® chair, clock kit • DecoArt™
   paint, varnish

Note: *Refer to color photos for
application and placement. Let paint,
varnish, and glue dry between
applications.*

VIVIAN PERITTS
SITTING PRETTY

FINISHED SIZE: 4½" X 10" X 4½"

All types and sizes of chairs are so popular. Now you can create one as a clock. Choose any paint colors to match your home décor.

INSTRUCTIONS

Please refer to Sitting Pretty pattern on page 102.

1. Use wood filler to fill any nail holes. Use sandpaper to lightly sand chair, wipe with tack cloth.
2. Use ¾" wash brush to apply one coat of White to entire chair.
3. Use ¾" wash brush to apply one coat of Light Buttermilk to entire chair.
4. Use ¾" wash brush to paint rungs and back Lemon Yellow.
5. To create upholstered look on seat, use sea sponge to apply Yellow Green to seat and edges.
   Note: *Sponge lightly, leaving areas of undercoat showing.*
6. Use #6 round brush with Blush Flesh to make irregular shaped flowers, painting some flowers over the edge of the sides as if seat were upholstered. Use round tip of brush to paint Lavender centers in each flower. See Figure #2.
   Note: *See Figure #1 for general size and shape of flowers.*

7. To create plaid on back of chair, use #4 flat brush to dry brush Yellow-Green vertical stripes approximately ½" apart. Dry brush Lavender horizontal stripes.
8. Paint all wooden beads Lavender. Glue one bead on bottom of each chair leg and one on top of each chair back.
9. Lightly spray several coats of the finisher/sealer to entire chair.
10. Use drill with bit to make ⅜" hole in center back of chair.
11. Attach clock movement and hands to chair following directions on back of packaging. Adhere numbers in place.

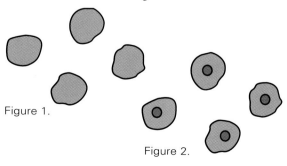

Figure 1.

Figure 2.

sitting pretty

Two 7" wooden clock circles*
Clock movement with hands for ¾"
    surface*
Acrylic paint*
    Opaque Red
    Persimmon
    Jubilee Green
    Lime Green
    Spice Brown
    White
All-purpose sealer*
Satin interior varnish *
Thick craft glue*
Two jumbo craft sticks
Two 8" x ³⁄₁₆" dowels
12" of 24 gauge wire
18" of ¼" thick cork
⅛ yard red check fabric
Brushes—#12 flat, #1 liner, #6 flat, 1"
    flat

Cotton swabs, drill with small bit,
    graphite paper, hammer and 1" small
    nails, palette or plate for paint, pencil,
    pinking shears, quarter, sanding
    sponge block, scissors, tracing paper,
    transfer paper

*These products were used: Walnut
Hollow® clock circles and clock
movement with hands • Delta
Ceramcoat® paint, sealer, varnish •
Sobo® glue

Note: *Refer to color photo for
application and placement. Let paint,
varnish, and glue dry between
applications.*

CHERYL BALL—COURTESY OF DELTA TECHNICAL COATINGS
CHERRY TIME

FINISHED SIZE: 18" X 13¾"

*You'll never be late again when you have this
handy clock and cork board. Just pin your
notes on the cork. This is an easy painting
project that can be finished in a day and used
year round.*

INSTRUCTIONS

Please refer to Cherry Time pattern on page 109.

1. To seal wood, use 1" flat brush to apply one coat sealer to clock circles and dowels. Sand smooth when dry with sanding sponge block.

2. To basecoat clock circles, use 1" flat brush to apply two coats Opaque Red.

3. To cut leaves and circle from cork, trace leaf shapes and one 6" circle onto cork. Use scissors to carefully cut out shapes.

4. Use 1" brush to apply Jubilee Green to larger leaves and jumbo craft sticks, Lime Green to smaller leaves, Persimmon to cork round, and Spice Brown to dowels.

5. To make leaves, apply glue to back of Lime Green leaves, smoothing and working glue to edges with finger. Position Lime Green leaves onto larger Jubilee Green leaves; press to secure. Glue one jumbo craft stick to back of each leaf, leaving 2" stem. Continue with other leaf. Glue cork circle to one wooden clock circle. To keep cork from curling, weigh down with books until dry.

6. To create small circles for numbers on clock, trace around a quarter, spacing evenly around clock circle. Use #6 flat brush with Persimmon to paint each circle and stripes around outside edges of both rounds and top edge next to cork.

7. Use cotton swabs dipped into paint to create dots. Place White dots on cork, Persimmon dots on clock, and Jubilee Green dots on leaves.

8. For clock numbers, use pencil to write numbers lightly on clock. Use #1 liner brush with White to paint numbers. Add dot at ends of each number by dipping wooden end of brush into White paint. Paint hands of clock White.

9. To varnish all pieces, use #1 flat brush to apply two coats of Satin Varnish.

cherry time

10. Use drill to make two small holes at one end of each dowel and a single hole 1" from top on other dowel and jumbo craft sticks.

11. To attach all pieces together, use wire. Line up single holes of tongue depressors and dowels. Thread wire through holes and twist around all parts to secure. Adjust dowel stems to backs of clock circles. Add dot of glue to dowel and hammer nails into place.

12. For fabric bow, use pinking shears to cut two strips of fabric, one 1½" x 12" and one 1½" by 24". Apply glue to one end of 12" piece and press onto junctions of stems and leaves. Wrap the remaining fabric around juncture to secure. Glue end down. Tie loopy bow with remaining piece of fabric, trim ends, and glue into place.

13. Attach clock movement and hands following directions on back of packaging.

MATERIALS

Basswood plank*
Clock movement and hands for ¾"
   surface*
Felt*: 5" x 14" Cashmere Tan
   9" x 12" sheets Sage, Denim,
   Sandstone, Butterscotch
   Scrap Walnut
Black embroidery floss
⅛ yard iron-on backing
Three small rocks
Acrylic paint: Blue
Black spray paint
Spray matte varnish
Fabric glue*
Easel for display (optional)

1" or wider brush, compass, drill with
⅜" bit, embroidery needle, palette,
pencil, rag, ruler, scissors, straight
pins, tracing paper

* These products were used: Walnut
Hollow® plank, clock movement with
hands • Kunin Rainbow™ felt •
Beacon® glue

Note: Refer to photos for application
and placement. Let paint, varnish, and
glue dry between applications.

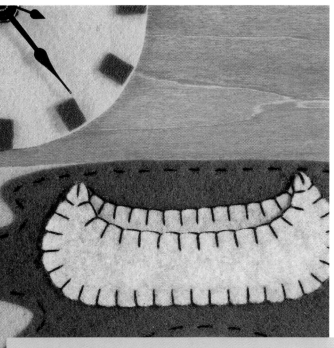

CHRIS MALONE
CABIN TIME

FINISHED SIZE: 9-11" X 13"

*This wooden plank clock features a simple
felt scene suitable for a lodge or den. Simple
stitches embellish some of the appliqués,
and real stones are attached to the scene.
Tell time by the "moon."*

INSTRUCTIONS

Please refer to Cabin Time pattern on page 107.

1. To stain top of board for sky, thin Blue paint with water. Use brush to apply paint to top 5 inches of board and immediately wipe off excess paint with rag so grain shows through. When dry, spray with two light coats of matte varnish.

2. Use patterns to cut out two trees from Sage felt, tree trunk from Walnut, lake from Denim, and canoe front and back from Sandstone.

3. Pin two trees together and blanket stitch edges with two strands of black floss. Blanket stitch top edge of two canoe pieces. Place canoe front on top of canoe back, matching bottom edges, and pin. Blanket stitch outside edges together. If desired, cut a slim piece of felt, about ⅛" wide and 2½" long, and slip inside canoe bottom to hold canoe slightly open at top.

4. For the ground, cut 5" x 14" piece of iron-on backing, and follow manufacturer's directions to apply to one side of Cashmere Tan felt. Place tracing paper over front of plank and trace bottom line between bark border and finished wood. Trace side edges and draw a gently curved line across top with sides about 3¾" high and center about 4" high. Use this pattern to cut out felt. (Reverse pattern and draw cutting lines on backing side.) Pin Denim lake to top of felt ground, matching top edges, and sew around lake with a running stitch using two strands of black floss.

5. Glue ground to bottom half of plank. Position tree on right side of plank, overlapping edge of lake. Place trunk under bottom edge of tree and glue tree and trunk in place. Glue canoe to lake and rocks to base of tree.

6. For clock face, cut 4" square from iron-on backing and apply to one side of Butterscotch felt. Cut a 3¾" circle. Cut out

12 small pieces of Walnut felt, about ¼" x ⅜", for hour markings. Space these rectangles evenly around edge of clock face; glue in place.

7. Spray clock hands with black paint.

8. Drill hole with ⅜" bit for clock movement approximately 3⅜" from left edge of plank,

centered between top of ground and top edge of sky. Cut hole in center of clock face large enough for shank of clock. Glue clock face to plank, matching holes.

9. Attach clock movement and hands following directions on back of packaging.
Optional: Display clock on easel.

cabin time

MATERIALS

Wood watering can*
Clock movement with hands*
Flower sponge & template*
Fabric brush set*: #1 Round Scrubber
   #4 Shader
   Stencil Size ¼
   #5/0 Spotter
¾" wash brush*
Acrylic paint*:
   Cool White
   Soft Lilac
   Orchid
   Royal Fuchsia
   Baby Pink
   Citron Green
   Wild Orchid
   Festive Green
   Light Parchment
Pen and ink* .30 tip, black ink
Plastic Fun Wire*: 20 gauge Icy Grape
Gesso spray*
Crystal Clear Varnish*

Drill with ¹⁄₁₆" and ³⁄₈" bits, fine grade
   sandpaper, paper plates, paper
   towels, scissors, tack cloth

* These products were used: Walnut
   Hollow® wood, clock movement •
   Loew-Cornell® sponge and template,
   brushes • DecoArt™ paint •
   KOH-I-NOOR® Rapidograph pen, ink
   • Toner® wire • Krylon® gesso
   spray, Crystal Clear Varnish

Note: *Refer to color photos for
application and placement. Let paint,
varnish, and glue dry between
applications.*

CAROLYN STEARNS

TIME TO WATER MY GARDEN

FINISHED SIZE: 7⅞" X 6⅛"

It is not necessary to be a decorative painter to create this wonderful, whimsical clock. For this free-form design, just use simple tools, paint, and wire, and then you really will have time to water your garden!

INSTRUCTIONS

1. Sand watering can with fine sandpaper, wipe with tack cloth.
2. To prime watering can, apply one coat Gesso spray. Sand lightly, wipe with tack cloth.
3. To basecoat watering can, use ¾" wash brush to apply one coat Cool White.
4. To create outside border, place plastic template ½" inside edge. Use stencil brush with Soft Lilac to paint border from template edge to outer edge of watering can, moving template around edge to complete.
5. To create flowers, place Light Parchment on paper plate. Dip flower sponge into paint, use flat brush to spread paint evenly on sponge.
   Note: *Test flower on paper plate. Add or remove excess paint.*
6. Begin making flowers by pressing flower sponge onto watering can in random pattern. Let some flowers go off edge. Add leaves with sponge using Festive Green.
7. Lay plastic template over flowers and leaves. Use #1 scrubber and 5/0 spotter to fill in lines using several colors. When the flowers are dry, fill in the leaves with Festive Green. ***Note:*** *Template will not fit exactly.*
8. Using pen and ink, add dot/dash line work to outline border, leaves, flowers.
9. To set ink, spray with one very light coat of Krylon Crystal Clear Varnish. When dry, spray with two more light coats.
10. To add wire, drill five ¹⁄₁₆" holes in spout of watering can. Cut piece of Fun Wire 24" long. Curl wire around paintbrush. Pull coils apart slightly. Cut five pieces of wire in different lengths: 1", 2", 3", 4", 5". Glue into holes. Trim as necessary.
11. Drill ³⁄₈" hole in center of watering can. Attach clock movement and hands following directions on back of packaging.

time to water my garden

MATERIALS

Lodge House birdhouse*
Clock movement with pendulum and
    hands*
Two 8½" x 11" sheets double-sided
    adhesive*
3 yards each flannel:
    Orange
    Yellow orange
    Red
2 yards Blue flannel
Small pieces of felt for appliqués

Craft thread, drill with ⅜" bit, hand
    needle, pencil, scissors, tracing paper

*These products were used: Walnut
    Hollow® birdhouse, clock movement
    with pendulum and hands •
    ThermoWeb® double-sided adhesive

Note: Refer to color photos for
application and placement.

LYNNE FARRIS
THATCHED COTTAGE

FINISHED SIZE: 6¾" X 11¼"(PLUS PENDULUM = 18½") X 5½"

This whimsical and colorful fabric art adaptation of a cuckoo clock is sure to become a favorite focal point for any casual décor. Easy to make, this clock is created from a simple wooden birdhouse, the roof is thatched with braids of brightly colored flannel strips, and the shingles are also created from flannel strips with colorful felt appliqués forming the clock face.

INSTRUCTIONS

1. Use scissors to cut all flannel into 1" strips.
2. Prepare birdhouse by drilling ⅜" hole in center of widest point of birdhouse front.
3. Use tracing paper and pencil to create pattern for roof, underside of front eaves, side walls, and front of birdhouse.
4. Transfer pattern to double-sided adhesive and cut out two roof pieces, two side wall pieces, and one front piece.
5. Remove paper backing from one surface of side wall pieces. Beginning at lower edge, place Blue strips so that they overlap approximately ¼", shingle style, until both side walls are covered. Trim along side edges.
6. Remove remaining paper backing and adhere to side walls of birdhouse.
7. Repeat same process with front wall. Use scissors to remove fabric and adhesive from ⅜" hole.
   Note: You will be covering both the original opening and your newly created hole.
8. Remove paper backing from double-sided adhesive roof and eave pieces to adhere to roof and underside of eaves. Remove other side of paper backing to expose adhesive surface.
9. Cut Orange, Yellow Orange, and Red flannel 1"-strips into 18-inch lengths. Using one strip of each color, braid together enough strips to cover roof of birdhouse, leaving ends free.
   Note: Use twist ties to secure braids temporarily until ready to adhere to clock.
10. Place braids close together vertically so that loose ends meet at tip of roof and hang over eaves slightly. Trim to fit. Adhere braids to front edges of roof and under eaves to complete the roof.
11. Attach clock movement following directions on back of packaging.
12. To create four clock face appliques, create simple flower shapes from felt, using contrasting color in center. Use craft thread and simple outline stitch to embellish, if desired. Adhere at four equidistant points on front of birdhouse to represent 12, 3, 6, and 9 o'clock.
13. Attach the pendulum to the clock movement.

thatched cottage

MATERIALS

Large open base pendulum clock*
Large pendulum clock movement*
Acrylic paint*:
    Black
    Pumpkin
    Peaches 'n Cream
    White
    Sand
    Viridian Green
    Olive Green
Three 4 oz. jars Magic Medium*
Magic Medium adhesive*
Magic Medium black leading*
Assorted beads: Black, Amber, Green
8' 16-gauge brass wire*
1 square foot heavy duty aluminum foil
12" x 12" Styrene Lighting Panel:
    Cracked Ice

Craft glue, drill with ⅛" bit, scissors,
pencil, needle nose pliers, waxed
paper

*These products were used: Walnut
Hollow® clock pendulum, clock
movement with hands • Deco Art™
paint, Magic Medium™, adhesive,
leading • Artistic Wire® wire

Note: *Refer to color photos for
application and
placement. Let paint,
varnish, and glue
dry between
applications.*

VIVIAN PERITTS
ART DECO

FINISHED SIZE: 7½" X 19¼" X 4"

*Magic Medium is a faux glass that comes in a
liquid formula. When prepared it can be cut
with scissors to any desired shape. It can be prepared
to create any color or combination of colors that you
desire and looks like the texture of glass.*

INSTRUCTIONS

Please refer to Art Deco pattern on pages 100 and 101.

1. Prepare three jars of Magic Medium in the
   following color combinations, following
   package instructions. Use two drops of each
   color for preparation. Pour mixture A on
   Styrene Panel, mixture B and C on waxed
   paper.
   A—Viridian Green and Olive Green
   B—Pumpkin and Peaches N Cream
   C—White and Sand
2. Use sponge brush to apply Black to entire
   clock.
3. For clock face, loosely ball up and smooth
   out foil. Place foil over clock face, use pencil
   to trace pattern onto foil. Use scissors to cut
   out face. Use craft glue to adhere foil, shiny
   side up, to clock face.
4. Use scissors to cut dried Magic Medium into
   shapes from pattern following colors
   designated on pattern. Use adhesive to
   adhere designs to top of foil on clock face.

Note: Each design section can consist of several

*pieces of Magic Medium, as if using real
stained glass.*

5. Follow package directions to apply black
   leading to clock face and edges.
6. Cut pieces of remaining prepared Magic
   Medium into approximately ½" squares,
   triangles, and rectangles.
7. Use drill with bit to create holes for wire, see
   Pattern B for wire lengths.
8. Use the needle nose pliers to curl one end of
   each wire. Add beads as indicated on
   pattern. Add craft glue to straight end of
   wire and insert into drilled holes.
9. Attach clock movement and hands following
   directions on back of packaging.
10. Following pattern for pendulum, adhere cut
    and dried Magic Medium pieces to
    pendulum with adhesive. Foil is not used
    this time. Add black leading.
11. Attach the pendulum to the clock
    movement.

art deco

MATERIALS

Wood tray*
Clock bezel movement*
Acrylic paints*:
    Light Avocado
    Light Buttermilk
    Dark Chocolate
Crackling medium*
Acrylic spray sealer*
Solid brass stencil*: Cameo
Brush*: 1" brush
Silk sea sponge*
Hot glue gun and glue sticks*
5½" white doily
30" length of 1" sheer, wire-edged
    ribbon to match
Gold spoon (or spray paint spoon gold)
Photo
Silk flowers to match cup and saucer
Tea bag
Tea cup, saucer

Double-stick tape, hammer, sawtooth
    hanger, stencil sponge

*These products were used: Walnut
    Hollow® tray bezel, clock movement
    • DecoArt™ paint, spray sealer,
    crackling medium • American
    Traditional™ stencil • Adhesive
    Tech™ hot glue gun, glue sticks •
    Loew-Cornell® shader brush, silk sea
    sponge

Note: *Refer to color photos for
application and placement. Let paint,
varnish, and glue dry between
applications.*

CRAFT MARKETING CONNECTIONS
VINTAGE TEA

FINISHED SIZE: 7¾" X 3" X 7¾"

Create a clock to remind you to set aside time for some of the smaller pleasures in life. The crackled-finish box, vintage photo, and antique cup and saucer will remind you of days gone by and is a perfect place to display a family heirloom.

INSTRUCTIONS

1. To basecoat tray, use 1" brush to apply one coat Light Avocado.
2. To crackle tray, use sea sponge filled with crackle medium. Apply to tray with dabbing motion covering entire tray. Follow label instructions for dry times.
3. For interior of tray, use 1" brush to apply one coat of Light Avocado over crackle medium. For exterior of tray, use 1" brush to apply one coat of Light Buttermilk.
4. To varnish entire tray, spray with sealer. *Note: The Cameo brass stencil itself is used as a frame for the photograph.*
5. To make stencil look old, use silk sea sponge to apply Dark Chocolate to stencil. Varnish stencil frame with spray sealer.

6. To attach sawtooth hanger, center on back of tray along top edge, hammer in place.
7. Assemble items to go into tray. Use double-stick tape to attach photo to back of stencil frame, allowing background of tray to show through stencil frame openings. Use hot glue to attach frame to upper right-hand corner of tray, silk flowers to the upper left-hand corner, plate vertically in front of flowers, doily to right side base of tray, cup and spoon to doily, tea bag in cup, silk flowers on both sides of indentation at top of tray. Tie ribbon into a bow, glue to top of tray, with bow streamers to sides of tray.
8. Gently wedge clock bezel movement into indentation on tray.

vintage tea

MATERIALS

Small regulator clock*
4 decorative corner pieces*
Fleur-de-lis decorative piece*
Clock pendulum movement with
    hands*
Arabic adhesive clock face, medium*
Acrylic paint*:
    French Blue
    Blue Ribbon
    Buttercup
    Hauser Green Dark
    Apple Spice
Satin spray varnish*
Brushes*: ¾" wash, #3 round, #1 liner

1" sponge brush, craft glue, fine
    sandpaper, paper towels, tack cloth,
    water container, wax paper palette,
    wood sealer

*These products were used: Walnut
    Hollow® clock, Classic Dimensions
    decorative wood pieces, clock
    movement with hands, adhesive
    clock face • Plaid® paint, varnish •
    Loew-Cornell® brushes

Note: *Refer to color photos for
application and placement. Let paint,
varnish, and glue dry between
applications.*

CHRIS WALLACE

FRENCH PROVINCIAL

FINISHED SIZE: 8¼" X 8¼" X 1¼"

*Add wonderful color and charm to any room
with a French Provincial look. It's easy to
attach decorative wood pieces that give
dimension and interest.*

INSTRUCTIONS

1. To prepare clock, use sponge brush to apply
   one coat of sealer to entire clock. Sand
   lightly. Use ¾" wash brush to apply two
   coats French Blue to entire clock. Use ¾"
   wash brush to apply two coats of Buttercup
   to all classic dimensions. Use ¾" wash brush
   to apply a wash of Buttercup to adhesive
   clock face.

2. To paint veining details on clock, use #3
   round with Blue Ribbon.

3. Use #3 round to paint clock edges with Blue
   Ribbon.

4. To paint edge details on adhesive clock face,
   use #3 round with Apple Spice.

5. Decorate Classic Dimensions corner pieces
   using #3 round with Hauser Green Dark
   comma strokes and Apple Spice dots.
   Decorate fleur-de-lis using #3 round with
   Apple Spice detail.

6. Adhere clock face to surface. (See page 83.)
   Glue all Classic Dimensions wood pieces in
   place.

7. Spray entire clock with 2-3 coats of varnish.

8. Attach clock pendulum movement and hands
   following directions on back of packaging.

french provincial

MATERIALS

Quilt block candle plate*
Clock movement with hands for ⅜"
    surface*
14 count white Vinyl Aida*
Embroidery floss*: 726, 907, 3746,
    3607, and 911
Acrylic paint*:
    Magenta
    Leaf Green
    White
    Pink Quartz
    Lime Green
    Crocus Yellow
    Christmas Green
Satin varnish*
Brushes*: ½" flat glaze, 0 round and 4
    round
Fabric glue*
15 inches white satin cord
No. 24 tapestry needle

Fine sandpaper, sawtooth hanger,
    pencil, sharp scissors, tack cloth,
    wood screw, and screw driver

*These products were used: Walnut
    Hollow® candle plate, clock
    movement • Charles Craft® Vinyl
    Aida cloth • DMC® embroidery floss
    • Delta® paint, varnish • Loew-
    Cornell® brushes • Beacon® Fabric-
    Tac glue

Note: *Refer to color photos for
application and placement. Let paint,
varnish, and glue dry between
applications.*

PHYLLIS DOBBS
CROSS STITCH QUILT

FINISHED SIZE: 8" X 8" X ¾"

*A counted cross stitch clock combines cross
stitch and paint to create a quilt design in
contemporary colors.*

INSTRUCTIONS

Please refer to Cross Stitch Quilt pattern on pages 104 and 105.

1. Using 2 strands of floss, cross stitch design following chart. Cut out design following lines on chart.

2. Place clock movement centered inside recessed area. After marking place with pencil where movement will hang, screw in wood screw. Leave screw head ⅛" from surface to hang clock movement. Nail sawtooth hanger on back at center top.

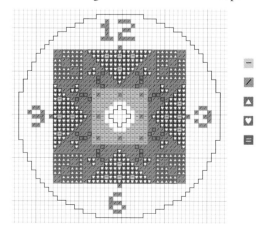

3. To prepare candle plate, lightly sand, wipe with tack cloth.

4. To basecoat candle plate, use ½" flat brush to paint recessed circle bottom and sides White. Use ½" flat brush and 4 round brush to paint sides and ¼" edge around top of candle plate Magenta. Use 0 round brush to paint flowers Magenta and stems and leaves Christmas Green. Paint small highlights on flowers Pink Quartz and on leaves Lime Green. Dip end of 0 round paint brush in Crocus Yellow paint to create dots.

5. Use ½" flat brush to apply two coats of satin varnish.

6. Use glue to adhere white satin cord to edge of cross stitch clock face. Place cross stitch clock face through shaft on front of clock movement. Add clock hands following directions on back of packaging. Hang movement on wood screw.

cross stitch quilt

MATERIALS

Butterfly shelter*
Clock movement*
Clock hands*
Three wood butterflies*
Four 1¼" ball knobs*
Stencil*: Delicate vine border
Sea sponge*
Fabric Brush Set*:
    #1 Round Scrubber
    #4 Shader
    Stencil Size ¼
    #5/0 Spotter
Brushes*:
    ¾" Wash Brush
    10/0 Liner
Acrylic paint *:
    Taffy Cream
    Marigold
    Cadmium Yellow
    Napa Red
    Hauser Light Green
    Hauser Medium Green
    Lamp Black
    Antique Gold
Faux glazing medium*
Gesso spray*
Crystal Clear Varnish*

Drill with ⅜" bit, fine sandpaper, paper
    plates, paper towels, pencil, Phillips
    screwdriver, tack cloth, tracing paper,
    transfer paper, water basin

*These products were used: Walnut
    Hollow® butterfly shelter, clock
    movement, clock hands, butterflies,
    ball knobs • Aleene's® glue • Loew-
    Cornell® brushes, sponge • Delta®
    stencil • DecoArt™ paint, medium •
    Krylon® gesso spray, spray varnish

Note: Refer to color photos for
application and placement. Let paint,
varnish, and glue dry between
applications.

CAROLYN STEARNS
TIME TO FLY

FINISHED SIZE: 6" X 13½" X 5½"

*Create a wonderful butterfly shelter with this
easy stencil and simple brush stroke
technique. Using background colors with
glaze you can create a soft-layered effect any
butterfly would like as a home!*

INSTRUCTIONS

Please refer to Time to Fly pattern on page 101.

1. To prime butterfly shelter and butterflies, lightly sand with fine sandpaper, wipe with tack cloth. Remove roof using Phillips screwdriver. Spray entire butterfly shelter with Gesso Spray.

2. Basecoat butterfly shelter using ¾" wash brush with Taffy Cream. Basecoat roof, ball knobs with Hauser Light Green.

3. Use paper plate to mix approximately one teaspoon each Marigold and Faux Glazing Medium. Wet sea sponge, squeezing out excess water. Dip sea sponge in mixture; blot off on paper plate. Start pressing the mixture onto the butterfly shelter, working one side at a time. Blot excess off with paper toweling. Use sea sponge to rub mixture in a circular motion to soften finish.

4. Use paper plate to mix approximately ½ teaspoon each Cadmium Yellow and Faux Glaze Medium. Use sponge to lightly apply mixture to all sides to add highlights.

5. Use paper plate to mix approximately ½ teaspoon each Hauser Medium Green and Faux Glaze Medium. Use sponge to apply to roof, ball knobs.

6. With stencil in place, use stencil brush with Hauser Light Green to stencil vine design on butterfly shelter, wrapping stencil around corners so design flows over entire area. To give depth to some leaves, use stencil brush to apply Hauser Medium Green to leaves in areas closest to vines as desired.

7. Stencil flowers with Napa Red. Add extra flowers here and there to give the butterfly shelter more color.

8. To give butterfly shelter a more hand-painted appearance, use 10/0 liner brush with Hauser Medium Green to loosely outline leaves. Paint a center vein on each leaf.

time to fly

9. Use ¾" wash brush to paint clock hands Napa Red.

10. Glue knobs to bottom corners.

11. To varnish, spray butterfly shelter and clock hands with 2-3 light coats of clear varnish.

12. Drill ⅜" hole in center of butterfly shelter. Attach clock movement and hands following directions on back of package.

13. Attach roof. Use brush to paint screw heads Hauser Light Green.

14. To basecoat butterflies, use ¾" wash brush to apply Antique Gold. On paper plate, mix 10 drops of Taffy Cream and 10 drops of glaze. Use sea sponge to lightly apply mixture onto butterflies.

15. After tracing pattern with pencil, use graphite paper to apply pattern onto butterflies. Use 10/0 liner to paint edges Napa Red; large spots Lamp Black. Liner and small dots on bottom butterfly are Taffy Cream; middle butterfly Hauser Light Green; top butterfly Cadmium Yellow.

16. Spray butterflies with 2-3 light coats clear varnish. Glue to shelter.

Wooden clock with bezel*
Transparent shiny paint*:
    White Pearl
    Citrine Yellow
    Crystal Orange
    Berry Quartz
    Sapphire
    Peridot
    Emerald
    Black Onyx
White Liquid Lead*
White glue*
32 gauge silver embossing metal*
#12 flat brush

Cardboard, craft stick, graphite paper, masking tape, palette, pencil, plastic disposable cup, ruler, scissors, straight pin, tracing paper

*These products were used: Walnut Hollow® clock with bezel • Delta® Paint Jewels™ • AMACO® embossing metal

Note: *Refer to color photos for application and placement. Let paint, varnish, and glue dry between applications.*

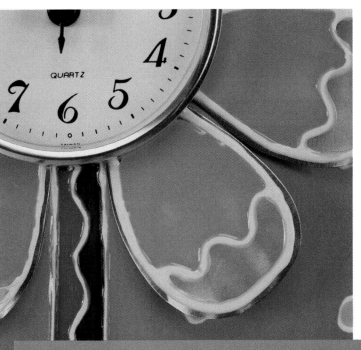

CHERYL BALL—COURTESY OF DELTA TECHNICAL COATINGS
FLOWER POWER

FINISHED SIZE: 9" X 12"

Use a fun type of transparent paint that is shiny when dry to create a Flower Power Clock for any room. It is easy, and the wood and metal need no surface preparation. After adding the petals, bend them up for a great dimensional look.

INSTRUCTIONS

Please refer to Flower Power pattern on page 109.

1. To prepare clock, remove clock movement. Use ruler and pencil to mark a ½" wide border around outside front edge. Mark 1" segments within border, adjusting to fit.

2. Trace stem and leaf pattern onto tracing paper with pencil. Position on clock and tape to secure. Transfer pattern by slipping graphite paper between pattern and clock, and retrace lines. Lightly pencil random dots on clock.

3. Trace flower petal on paper with pencil, cut. Roll metal flat. Trace around petal shape on metal to make 8 petals and cut. Make small roll of masking tape, attach to back of each petal, press securely on cardboard.

4. Use White Liquid Lead paint to outline clock and petals.

5. To fill in petals, squeeze paint into center of sections, using tip of bottle to work paint to edges. Add more paint as needed to fill in areas, but do not overfill. Work in alternate areas on design, letting areas dry slightly before continuing as follows: White Pearl for alternate border squares; Black Onyx for border squares; Crystal Orange for lower part of petal; Citrine Yellow for upper part of petals, dots; Peridot for half of stem, sections on leaves; Emerald for stem, section of leaves,

6. To mix light blue background, squeeze White Pearl into plastic cup, add a few drops of Sapphire, and stir with craft stick. Continue adding Sapphire until desired color is created. Make enough for entire

area. Pour small amount into a section on background and smooth with flat brush. Continue until background is complete.

7. To paint side of clock, place Berry Quartz onto palette. Use #12 flat brush to apply two coats of paint.

8. Remove dried petals from cardboard, remove masking tape rolls from backs, and position petals around opening of clock. Apply glue to back lower edge of each petal and press onto clock. Insert clock bezel when dry.

PAINT TIPS:

TO MIX PAINT IN BOTTLE, ROLL BOTTLE SEVERAL TIMES ON WORK SURFACE. SNIP TIP OF BOTTLE. SQUEEZE SMALL AMOUNT OF PAINT INTO EACH SECTION, MOVE PAINT TO EDGES WITH BOTTLE TIP, ADDING MORE AS NEEDED TO FILL SECTION. IF SECTION IS OVERFILLED, REMOVE EXCESS WITH DAMP COTTON SWAB. KEEP FIRM PRESSURE ON BOTTLE FOR EVEN LINES. KEEP TIP OF BOTTLE CLEAN BY WIPING WITH PAPER TOWEL BETWEEN SECTIONS. USE STRAIGHT PIN TO POP ANY BUBBLES THAT MAY FORM IN PAINT.

flower power

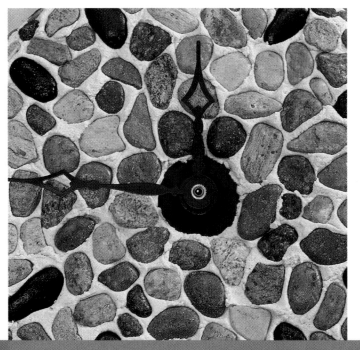

MATERIALS

Clock movement for ¾" surface*
Black clock hands*
Hold the Foam Glue*
1" x 6" disc Styrofoam*
No-prep metal paint*: Black
Premixed ceramic tile adhesive & grout
Large pebble aquarium gravel
Two 6" x ¼" dowels
6" circle of black felt

Brush, butter knife, cotton swabs, craft
   knife, fabric marker, pencil, plastic
   cup, ruler, scissors, toothpicks

*These products were used: Walnut
   Hollow® clock movement, hands •
   Dow® Chemical Company foam disc
   • Deco Art™ metal paint • Beacon®
   Chemical Company glue

Note: *Refer to color photos for
application and placement. Let paint,
adhesive, grout, and glue dry between
applications.*

KOREN RUSSELL

ROCK AROUND THE CLOCK

FINISHED SIZE: 6½" X 1¼"

Cutting Styrofoam and squishing pebbles into mud is like child's play. Relax and let the time slip away as you create this rustic clock. Hang it on the wall or follow the instructions to make a wood dowel stand.

INSTRUCTIONS

1. Select 12 large rocks to use for the hour positions. Use brush to paint tops and sides black.
2. Use ruler to find center of disc, push pencil through foam at center point. Remove parts from shaft of clock movement, set aside. Push shaft of clock movement through hole.
3. Use pencil to trace around outside of back of clock movement onto disc. Remove clock movement from disc. Use craft knife to cut along traced pencil lines. Use butter knife to chip out ½" depth of foam where clock movement will be placed. *Note: The shaft will stick out ¼" from front of clock when ½" of foam is removed.*
4. Attach clock movement and hands following directions on back of package.
5. Locate triangle-shaped hanger on back of clock movement. Following point of triangle straight up, place toothpick into side of foam disc to mark top of clock.
6. Move clock hands to bottom of clock. Working by either holding clock or setting onto plastic cup, use butter knife to spread ¼" layer of grout onto face of clock, beginning between 11 o'clock and 4 o'clock positions. Spread grout to just short of rubber cushion. When pebbles are pressed into place, grout will squish to edge of rubber cushion. Continue working to complete entire clock face.
7. Place painted pebbles in hour positions near edge of disc, moving clock hands to help visualize placement.
8. Remove toothpick and spread ¼" thick grout on side edges of disc. Using flat pebbles, press firmly into grout, filling between hour pebbles. Use cotton swabs to clean off any grout on tops of pebbles and rubber cushion.
9. Spread thick layer of grout to wrap around disc to ½" on back.
   Note: Allow the grout to dry for 12-24 hours.
10. Center felt on back of disc. Remove felt from area where clock movement will be placed, trimming circle as necessary. Glue in place. Replace clock movement and hands.

rock around the clock

Optional Dowel Stand

1. To mark where dowel stand will be inserted, measure 1" from top point of triangle hanger and lightly place a mark, then mark ½" to each side. Using craft knife, cut a ¼" "X" in felt. Push dowels through felt, ¾" into disc at 90 degree angle. Check to see clock stands properly. Bottoms of dowels can be trimmed at an angle so they sit flat on surface.

2. Remove dowels, paint Black. Place glue on ends of dowels and push into holes.

Doll furniture bench*
3" bezel movement*
Velvet pigskin suede*: Gold, Purple
Cowhide suede (8½" x 11" trim piece)*:
   Red
3 yards 1mm black round lace*
Polymer mallet and punch board *
Fourteen ³⁄₃₂" eyelets & setter*
7 (⁵⁄₆₄") round drive punch*
Rotary cutter, tiara decorative blade
Acrylic paint*: Light Foliage Green
Fabric paint*: Metallic Bronze
Satin varnish*
All-purpose sealer*
Stamp images*: 14-417S, 14084-D
Glass size 9 disc beads (2 each)
Glass pony beads (2 each)
#5 seed beads: transparent gold, light
   blue, green, and red
Nylon beading thread and Glover or
   Sharps needle

½" flat brush, 1" sponge brush, contact
   cement, cosmetic sponges, craft
   knife with extra #11 blades, drill with
   3" hole saw, fine sandpaper, hi-loft
   batting, pencil, poster board,
   scissors, straight edge ruler,
   toothpick

*These products were used: Walnut
   Hollow® bench, bezel movement •
   The Leather Factory® velvet pigskin
   suede, cowhide suede, mallet, board,
   eyelets, setter, round drive punch,
   round lace • Delta® paints, varnish,
   sealer • Magenta® stamps

Note: *Refer to color photos for
application and placement. Let paint,
varnish, and glue dry between
applications.*

KARI LEE
TAKE A SEAT

FINISHED SIZE: 10½" X 10¼" X 4½"

*Transitional, eclectic, or somewhere in between, this is a
clock created with a passion for color and a statement of
individuality. A smooth application of foliage green
paint sets the stage for the rubberstamped, passionate
purple and red suede bench back drape and seat
cushion. Accents of eyelets, beads, black round lace, and
handmade suede tassels complete the declaration for
independence of time.*

INSTRUCTIONS

Please refer to Take a Seat pattern on page 98.

1. To prepare bench, use ruler to determine center on back, mark with pencil. Drill 3" hole with saw blade. Use sandpaper to smooth away rough edges around hole and over entire bench.

2. Use 1" sponge brush to apply sealer to entire bench. Sand lightly. Use 1" sponge brush to apply two coats of Light Foliage Green paint and one coat of varnish to surface.

3. Transfer bench back pattern onto poster board. Use craft knife to cut pattern, remove 3" clock circle. Save circle for later. Use straight edge ruler with pencil to create a 4" x 10½" seat cushion pattern from poster board, cut out.

4. Using craft knife and poster board seat back pattern, cut pattern out of red cowhide suede with 3" hole on top side of suede. Cut four 2⅛" x 4" strips from purple pig suede. Cut one decorative edge along length of each strip using a straight edge as guide and rotary cutter equipped with tiara decorative blade.

Note: *Great care was taken to match the decorative cut pattern on each cut strip so they would match.*

5. Secure strips with contact cement to underside of seat cover's outside edges, overlapping strips approximately ¼". Place seat cover onto punch board, and using a ⁵⁄₆₄" round drive punch with mallet, punch five holes needed along all four decorative cut edges of purple suede for eyelets to be attached. Place ³⁄₃₂" eyelets in punched holes from top side of seat cover. Use eyelet setter to secure eyelets.

6. To stamp image, apply an even coat of Metallic Bronze paint onto large stamp with a cosmetic sponge. Stamp image onto a piece of purple pig suede. Cut around image with craft knife. Position 3" poster board circle in center of stamped image and, using it as a guide, cut out circle. Position circle around clock opening, secure with contact cement.

7. Cut two 24" lengths of 1mm black round lace. Position seat cover onto seat back. Thread center of one lace length between top two eyelet holes along top edge from underside. Thread each lace end to next eyelet on opposite side, overlapping lace to create pattern. Continue this step until reaching bottom edge. Secure lace ends together with an overhand knot. Repeat on other side of seat cover.

8. To create tassels for bottom of lace ends, cut two 1" x 1½" rectangles from gold pig suede. Using a craft knife, cut ⅞" long fringe along one 1½" length leaving ⅛" margin along top of rectangle. Once first fringe piece has been cut, repeat step on other gold rectangle. Thread a glass pony bead on one knotted lace end. Apply a small amount of contact cement along backside of one margin of fringe. Wrap fringe around knot and hold until secure. Repeat step for other tassel.

9. To create purple suede seat cushion, place two 5" x 11½" purple suede trim pieces wrong sides together on cutting surface. Center 4" x 10½" seat cushion pattern on layered suede pieces. Using a straight edge as an additional guide and a rotary cutter equipped with a tiara decorative blade, cut out top and bottom matching seat cushion covers. Use scissors to cut 3" x 9½" rectangle from high loft batting. Use contact cement between cut batting on backside and center of one suede cover.

10. Use smaller stamp with metallic bronze paint applied with cosmetic sponge to create two images, three inches apart and centered between 5" width of seat cushion. Allow to dry.

11. On backside of both covers apply thin, even coat of cement ½" from decoratively cut edges. Place wrong sides of covers together, sandwiching batting between. Align edges and press together to secure.

12. To create contours in cushion surface, known as a tuft, begin by using Glovers or Sharps needle and length of nylon beading thread attached. Stitch through underside of seat cushion and up through center of one stamped image, leaving a 4" length of thread on underside. Thread one disc bead followed by one seed bead onto needle. Thread needle back through disc bead and back to underside of seat cushion, bypassing seed bead. Thread one seed bead onto needle and thread. Pull thread ends tightly, secure with a double knot made around bead. Repeat this step to create remaining tuft.

13. In each corner of seat cover, through both layers of suede, punch one ⁵⁄₆₄" hole. Attach ³⁄₃₂" eyelet in each corner hole. Cut two 12" and two 16" lengths of black round lace. Position tufted cushion onto bench. Thread a 12" lace length through one back corner hole and wrap lace around adjoining bench leg and secure with overhand knot. Secure remaining back corner of cushion with lace in same manner. Cut excess lace away.

14. Use 16" lengths of lace to secure front two corners of cushion onto bench, securing lace with overhand knot and leaving excess lace for additional embellishment. Thread several beads onto each lace length and secure with an overhand knot.

15. To create tassels for ends of lace, cut four 1" squares from gold suede. Cut fringe along one edge of squares, leaving a ⅛" margin along top. Apply cement to margin on underside of fringe piece. Wrap fringe around one end knot, securing beads. Repeat for remaining three lace ends.

16. Insert bezel movement into hole of bench seat back from front.

   Note: If space is at a premium, this fine piece of furniture can hang on the wall with the addition of picture hanging hardware.

take a seat

MATERIALS

Wood clock*
Clock movement for ¾" surface*
Acrylic paint and mediums*:
   Asphaltum
   Warm White
   Green Umber
   Parchment
   Coffee Bean
   Iridescent Gold
Paint mediums*:
   Glazing
   Blending gel
   Water-base varnish
Brushes*: #12, 16 flat, #1 liner
Palette*
Roll ¾" transparent tape*

1" sponge brush, 100% cotton rags or soft paper towels, brush basin, fine grade sandpaper, graphite paper, green scrubber, old toothbrush, pencil, piece of brown paper bag with no printing, palette knife, stylus, tack cloth, tracing paper, utility palette

*These products were used: Walnut Hollow® wooden clock, clock movement with hands • Plaid® paints, mediums • Masterson's® Sta-Wet Palette • Loew-Cornell® brushes • 3M® transparent tape

Note: *Refer to color photos for application and placement. Let paint, varnish, and glue dry between applications.*

PRISCILLA HAUSER
SAND DOLLARS

FINISHED SIZE: 9" X 9" X ¾"

This hallway, kitchen, or bathroom clock features sea urchins, better known as sand dollars, hand-painted on the surface. So fragile are these little creatures that they live on the sandy bottom of the sea.

INSTRUCTIONS

Please refer to Sand Dollars pattern on page 111.

1. Sand clock with fine grade sandpaper, wipe with tack cloth.
2. To basecoat, use 1" sponge brush to apply two coats of Parchment.
3. Use ruler and tape to create stripes. Apply strips of tape, leaving ¾" spaces between each strip.
4. Use 1" sponge brush to lightly apply Coffee Bean in open spaces of taped area. Remove tape.
5. To give surface an old look, use wet green scrubber to sand Coffee Bean stripes. Wipe thoroughly with damp cloth. Sand clock with piece of brown paper bag with no printing. Wipe with tack cloth.
6. After tracing pattern with pencil, transfer pattern to clock using stylus and placing graphite paper between pattern and clock.
7. Use #12 flat brush to undercoat each sand dollar with two to three coats Warm White, leaving center star design unpainted.
8. Use #12 flat to apply wash of Parchment to centers. Add a light Green Umber wash also to each center.
9. Reapply the pattern to undercoated sand dollars.
10. Use #1 liner with Green Umber to outline details to center star of each sand dollar. Add wash of Green Umber also.
11. Use #12 brush and a mix of Asphaltum and Green Umber to darken wash around center. Use very little color.
12. Using #16 flat brush filled with Blending Gel, lightly shadow background by applying a wash of Green Umber and Asphaltum. Add more shadows around lower right background areas of each sand dollar, shading from darker (close to the sand dollar) to lighter as color blends away from sand dollar. Use same colors to shade area where sand dollars overlap and around design in center.

sand dollars

13. Use #16 flat brush, mixed with Blending Gel, to apply wash of Iridescent Gold to two back sand dollars. Use #1 liner of Iridescent Gold to outline other three sand dollars.

14. Spatter entire surface using old toothbrush filled with mix of Green Umber and Asphaltum thinned with water. Use finger to pull back on bristles, holding toothbrush close to surface. Let paint spatters fall onto surface.

15. To varnish, use #16 flat brush to apply two coats of water base varnish.

16. Attach the clock movement and hands following directions on back of packaging.

MATERIALS

Creative Woodburner*
Mini Flow Point*
Corner shelf*
Clock movement for ¾" surface*
Gold clock hands*
Roman adhesive clock face*
Burnt Umber oil color pencil*
Acrylic paint *:
　Antique White
　Burnt Umber
　Dark Foliage Green
　Dusty Mauve
　Empire Gold
　Bungalow Blue
　Wedgwood Green
　White
　14K Gold Gleams
Mediums*
　Satin Interior Varnish
　Clear Glaze Base
　Crackle
Brushes*:
　# 3 and 6 rounds
　# 4 flat
　#1 liner
　¾" wash

No. 2 pencil, drill with ⅜" bit, fine sandpaper, foam plate, graphite transfer paper, heat-resistant surface (such as a cookie sheet), masking tape, needle-nose pliers, paper towels, scrap piece of wood for practice, small paper cup, soft large brush, tack cloth, toothpick

*These products were used: Walnut Hollow® woodburner and point, shelf, clock movement, hands, adhesive clock face, oil color pencil • Delta® paint and mediums • Loew-Cornell® brushes

Note: *Refer to color photos for application and placement. Let paint, varnish, and glue dry between applications.*

VICKI SCHREINER

FRESH FLOWERS CORNER SHELF

FINISHED SIZE: 18" X 4¾" X 9"

Create a unique clock that is useful as well as functional. Place this woodburned shelf in the corner to hold special treasures.

INSTRUCTIONS

Please refer to Fresh Flowers Corner Shelf pattern on page 99.

1. To prepare shelf, lightly sand, wipe with tack cloth. Use ¾" wash brush to basecoat top of shelf with two coats Antique White. In small paper cup, mix equal parts Antique White with water. Work on one side of shelf at a time. Use ¾" wash brush to apply mix to bottom section of shelf. Wipe off immediately with paper towels.

2. Follow label instructions to apply crackle to top of shelf. Using the ¾" brush, apply one even coat of crackle to top section of shelf with strokes going from left to right across shelf. Let dry until tacky, 15 to 40 minutes depending on humidity. Do not let dry completely. Brush on one light even coat of Wedgwood Green with strokes going from left to right across shelf. Avoid over-brushing or it will cause smearing. Top coat will begin to crack within minutes.

3. Transfer traced pattern to front on bottom section of shelf as follows: Lay patterns onto front of shelf and hold in place with small pieces of masking tape; slide graphite paper under patterns (graphite side down); trace designs using No. 2 pencil. Do not transfer stippled dots; these are shown for shading reference.

　Note: *Carefully follow manufacturer's safety instructions on package when using the wood-burning tool.*

4. Before plugging in woodburning tool, remove universal point and replace with mini flow point, tighten with needle nose pliers. Tape wire holder onto heat-resistant surface with masking tape. Place woodburning tool on holder, plug in, and allow to heat.

　Note: *Practice a few strokes on a piece of scrap wood before working on project. Use slow,* *small sketching strokes instead of long continuous strokes. Do not use heavy pressure. The length of time you keep the tip on the surface of the wood determines the darkness, not pressure. Let the heat do the work. To maintain even heat flow, keep the tip clean by frequently dragging it across fine sandpaper. Relax and have fun!*

5. Burn the outline of designs. Do not burn the small dot flowers. Do not burn the border stripe. Apply several random scattered dots throughout designs.
   Note: Use appropriate size brushes to fit the area you are painting.

6. On foam plate, mix equal parts Glaze Base with each color paint to create shear color that will not hide woodburning. Basecoat leaves with Wedgwood Green. Basecoat flower petals with White. Basecoat flower centers with Empire Gold.

7. On foam plate, mix equal parts Glaze Base with each color paint. Refer to original pattern and work on small areas at a time. Shade as follows: Load brush with small amount of paint. Stroke on palette to remove some of the paint. Dab paint in area to be shaded. Quickly dry brush on paper towel. Pat dry brush onto applied paint to blend and soften. Shade leaves with Dark Foliage Green. Shade flower petals with Dusty Mauve. Shade flower centers with Burnt Umber.

8. Using handle of paint brush, apply dots for small flowers. Dot flower petals with Bungalow Blue and centers with Empire Gold. Using a toothpick, apply tiny dot to right side of each small flower center with White. Using #1 liner brush, apply a small comma stroke to right side of each large flower center.

9. Basecoat border stripe across bottom of shelf with 14K Gold.

10. After all painting is completed, clean out all woodburned grooves by going along inside of each groove with Burnt Umber oil color pencil.

11. Spray two coats varnish to entire shelf.

12. Use drill with ⅜" bit to create hole for clock movement.

13. Adhere adhesive clock face to front of shelf. Attach clock movement and hands following directions on back of packaging.

fresh flowers
corner shelf

Wooden 6" circle plaque*
2¼" Clock Bezel Movement*
Wooden turnings*:
  ball knobs: five ¾", two 1", three 1¼",
    one 1½"
  Three ¾" pine blocks
  Three 1½" toy wheels
Fabric paint*: Gold Sparkles
Beads*: Size 2 bugles: Gunmetal,
  Opaque White, Fuchsia
  Size 3 twisted bugles: Light Blue,
  Amethyst
Size 11/0 seeds: Ruby Iris, Topaz-Pink,
  Yellow Lime, Purple-Aqua, Dk.
  Amethyst Iris, Ceylon Pink, Ceylon
  White AB, Black Matte, Aqua Matte,
  Iris
Size 11/0 seeds, transparents: Aqua
  Luster, Light Green Luster, Royal
  Blue
Size 11/0 seeds, opaques: Orange,
  Yellow Luster, Yellow-Orange Luster
Thick craft glue*

Acrylic paint, bead tray, brush, hook
  and loop tape (optional), hammer,
  long straight pen and/or needle tool,
  pencil, sawtooth or other hanging
  hardware

*These products were used: Walnut
  Hollow® plaque, wood turnings,
  clock bezel movement • Elizabeth
  Ward & Co., Inc. beads • Tulip®
  fabric paint • Crafter's Pick™ glue

Note: *Refer to color photos for
application and placement. Let paint
and glue dry between applications.*

CINDY GORDER
BEAD COLLAGED TIMEPIECE

FINISHED SIZE: 6" ROUND

*Unlike most beadwork, this project does not
require thread, complicated techniques or patterns.
If you can squeeze glue from a bottle, you can
create this clock!*

GENERAL TECHNIQUES

1. The fabric paint will act as "glue" for the beads. Squeeze fabric paint in small areas or short lines. Use a long straight pen, or needle tool, to pick up beads in the fabric paint with holes facing sideways, not up. Nudge beads close together using the end of the pin.

2. If there is excess paint around the beads, when dry, the glitter will blend in with the beads and enhance the overall look.

3. Keep surface somewhat horizontal until beads are set enough to stay in place. The fabric paint sets up fairly fast, so work several small areas at a time, making sure not to disturb any recently positioned beads. Reapply fabric paint as needed. Once fabric paint has hardened overnight, those areas with beading can be handled without disturbing the set beads.

4. Keep your tools clean by wiping often with paper towel. Also keep nozzle of fabric paint bottle clean.

bead collaged
timepiece

INSTRUCTIONS

1. To basecoat back of plaque, brush with any color acrylic paint. Use hammer to attach sawtooth hanger to back.

2. To make border around edge, squeeze a 1½" length of fabric paint, pick up an Opaque White bugle bead, set into fabric paint. Pick up another, set directly above first one. Pick up a third, set next to the first, add a fourth next to second one. Nudge all four beads close together. Repeat with four Gunmetal bugle beads continuing around edge, alternating colors. Continue working on edge, alternating color blocks to create checks.

3. After deciding on placement of clock bezel movement, wheels, balls, and cubes on plaque surface, set aside the clock bezel movement. Glue each wood turning in place.

4. Use fabric paint to cover the exposed areas of the plaque face with 11/0 transparent Aqua Luster and size 3 twisted Light Blue bugles. Cover ball knobs, wheels, and cubes with other beads as desired. To make a spiral design on ball knob, "draw" spiral with fabric paint in small sections, add beads, then fill in around it with beads of a different color. Make stripes in a similar manner. A simple design can be made by starting at the bottom of a ball and working up, alternating colors in every other row.

   Note: Leave the clock bezel movement out of the clock until all the beading is completed, but check the fit of the opening often. Areas of components touching the clock bezel movement may need to be left unbeaded.

5. Apply two rows of black and white seed beads to make checks around clock bezel movement lens. Insert into beaded wood turnings.

   Optional: Attach clock bezel movement to the plaque using hook and loop tape trimmed to fit back.

Wood clock*
Clock movement for ¾" surface with
    hands*
Acrylic paint*:
    Hauser Green Light
    Hauser Green Medium
    Green Umber
    Ice Green Light
    Titanium White
    Yellow Light
    True Burgundy
    Red Light
    Wicker White
    Licorice
    Fresh Foliage
    Calico Red
Paint mediums*:
    Blending gel
    Water-based varnish
Brushes*: # 2, 8, 12 flat, #1 liner, 1"
    wash brush
⅝" dauber*
Palette*
Roll ¾" transparent tape*

1" sponge brush, 100% cotton rags or
    soft paper towels, brush basin, fine
    grade sandpaper, graphite paper,
    pencil, piece of brown paper bag
    with no printing, palette knife, stylus,
    tack cloth, tracing paper, utility
    palette

*These products were used: Walnut
    Hollow® wooden clock, clock
    movement with hands • Plaid®
    paints, mediums, dauber •
    Masterson's® Sta-Wet Palette •
    Loew-Cornell® brushes • 3M®
    transparent tape

Note: *Refer to color photos for
application and placement. Let paint,
varnish, and glue dry between
applications.*

PRISCILLA HAUSER
GINGHAM & CHERRIES

FINISHED SIZE: 10¼" X 14¾" X ¾"

*This cherry clock can't help but brighten any
time of day. Its gingham background
complements the bright red cherries and their
leaves.*

INSTRUCTIONS

Please refer to Gingham & Cherries pattern on page 103.

1. Sand wood clock with fine grade sandpaper, wipe with tack cloth.

2. To basecoat, use 1" sponge brush to apply two or more coats of Wicker White. Rub with piece of brown paper with no printing to smooth nap of wood.

3. To create gingham look, apply strip of ¾" transparent tape vertically down center of wood clock. Continue applying strips of tape side-by-side on each side of center strip until entire face is covered with tape. Remove tape on either side of center strip and every other strip.
   Note: Rub remaining tape firmly to assure it is secure to surface.

4. Use #1 wash brush to apply one coat of thinned Licorice between tapes to create stripes. Remove tape before paint has completely dried.

5. Now apply strips of tape in opposite direction, horizontally. Remove every other strip of tape as described above, apply wash of Licorice, removing tape before paint has completely dried. If needed, rub with a piece of brown paper bag with no printing to smooth nap of wood.

6. Neatly trace cherries design with pencil. Transfer design using graphite paper between design and wood clock.

7. To paint leaves, use #12 flat brush to undercoat leaves with two or more coats of Fresh Foliage. Shade base of leaves with Green Umber. Working on one leaf at a time, apply Blending Gel to leaf. Apply Titanium White at the top of leaf, Hauser Green Medium or Hauser Green Light, and Yellow Light in the middle of leaf and Green Umber at base. Working quickly and using a

light touch, blend each leaf, pulling from bottom to top and then from top to bottom. *Note: The Blending Gel will keep the paint wet to give more time to blend the leaves.*

8. To paint cherries, use #8 flat to undercoat cherries with two or more coats of Calico Red.

9. To shade cherries, double load #8 flat brush with Blending Gel and True Burgundy. Blend on palette to soften colors. Apply to sides of cherries.

10. To add details to cherries, pick up Red Light on dauber, removing excess paint on paper towel. Dab the Red Light in center of cherry.

Apply a second coat if desired. Pick up Yellow Light on dauber, removing excess paint on paper towel, and add a highlight to the center of the cherry.

11. Shade indentations for stem areas by floating #2 flat brush with True Burgundy.

12. Using #1 liner brush, paint stem with Green Umber and Hauser Green Medium.

13. Use #1 wash brush to apply two to three coats of water base varnish to entire wood clock.

14. Attach clock movement and hands following directions on back of packaging.

gingham & cherries

Wood box*
Clock movement for ¾" surface with
    hands*
Wood embellishment*
Spray paints*:
    Moss Green
    Hill Green
    Glossy Wood Tones
    Mess Master*
    Clear Finish Sealer (matte)*
Two 1" x 1" corner braces
5" x 5½" piece of white cardstock
Tacky glue*
Hot glue gun and glue sticks*

Brush, cotton swabs, drill and ⅜" drill
    bit, handsaw, pencil, ruler, sea
    sponge, steel wool (optional)

*These products were used: Walnut
    Hollow® box, clock movement with
    hands, wood embellishment •
    Design Master® paint • Aleene's®
    tacky glue • Adhesive Tech™ hot
    glue gun, glue sticks

Note: *Refer to color photos for
application and placement. Let paint,
varnish, and glue dry between
applications.*

CRAFT MARKETING CONNECTIONS
DESK ORGANIZER

FINISHED SIZE: 9¾" X 6³⁄₁₆" X 7¼"

*Turn a wooden box into a sophisticated-looking
timepiece that will help keep your desk organized. The
use of spray paints makes this a quick and easy project.
Detailed carving on the wood embellishment provides
an attractive back-plate for the clock movement.*

INSTRUCTIONS

1. Use handsaw to cut knob from lid. Use drill with ⅜" drill bit to make hole in center of lid and wood embellishment.

2. In a well-ventilated area, spray box, cardstock, and braces with Moss Green paint. For sponged application of paint, spray Hill Green paint directly onto sponge and immediately apply to surface of box, cardstock, and braces, repeating process until all pieces are covered. For a more muted look, spray sponge with Moss Green paint and sponge over Hill Green.

3. To keep lid open, use hot glue to adhere braces on both sides to back of box, aligning with outside edges of box and lid. Spray entire box with Clear Finish Sealer.

4. In a well-ventilated area, heavily spray top of wood embellishment with Glossy Wood Tone paint, allowing paint to drip into crevices of wood. Before embellishment dries completely, spray a cotton swab with Mess Master and rub finish off top area of wood, leaving outer border and border around center medallion. Continue removing spray paint on raised areas until desired effect is achieved.

Optional: For a duller finish, lightly rub steel wool across surface of wood embellishment.

5. Use craft glue to adhere wood embellishment to inside of lid. To cover hinges, use brush to smooth glue onto back of painted cardstock. Press cardstock onto bottom side of open lid and down inside back of box.

6. Attach clock movement and hands following directions on back of packaging.

desk organizer

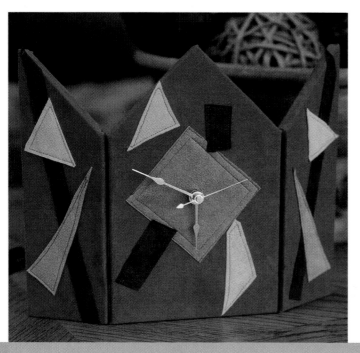

MATERIALS

Materials
Small Gothic Triptych*
Clock movement with hands for ¼"
  surface*
Two 8½" x 11" sheet of double-sided
  adhesive*
One 12" x 24" piece of fabric*
Several small pieces of fabric*

Drill with ⅜" bit, pencil, sewing
  machine, matching and contrasting
  threads, scissors, tracing paper

*These products were used: Walnut
  Hollow® Triptych, clock movement
  with hands • ThermoWeb® double-
  sided adhesive • Ultrasuede® fabric

Note: *Refer to color photos for
application and placement.*

LYNNE FARRIS

ULTRA-MODERN TRIPTYCH

FINISHED SIZE: 9" X 7¼" X ¼"

Ultra-modern, ultra chic! This stylish triptych clock features a contemporary collage created from luxurious Ultrasuede®. It would make the perfect gift for a man or can be used as a tabletop focal point in a contemporary décor.

INSTRUCTIONS

Prepare Triptych by drilling a ⅜" hole in center of center panel.

1. Use tracing paper to create patterns of 3 parts of Triptych adding ¼" around all sides. Transfer patterns onto double-sided adhesive.

2. Trace patterns onto solid Ultrasuede® pieces to form background for three sections of collage. Reverse patterns and trace onto remaining fabric to cover back side of Triptych.

3. Arrange Ultrasuede® pieces in pleasing patterns onto background. Sew around raw edges of collage pieces to attach to background.

4. Remove paper backing from one side of double-sided adhesive and smooth onto wrong side of collage pieces.

5. Remove remaining backing papers and smooth into place on Triptych, carefully folding around edges. Trim to fit at corners, and trim fabric away from drilled hole.

6. To cover back side, trim fabric with double sided adhesive to fit exactly on back sides of three panels. Remove paper backing and carefully adhere to back of Triptych, being sure to cover raw edges from front. Cut away fabric from around drilled hole.

7. Attach clock movement and hands following directions on back of packaging.

ultra-modern triptych

MATERIALS

Small open base clock*
Clock movement with hands for ¾"
 surface*
Gel stain (conditioner, stain, and
 finish)*: Aged Oak
Stencil Paint Cremes*:
 Barn Red
 Paprika
 Hunter Green
 Colonial Green
Acrylic paint*: Antique White
Goatskin parchment rawhide*
1 yard rawhide lace*
Two-prong lacing needle*
8½" x 11" piece of 2 to 3 oz. vegetable
 tanned natural leather*
⅛" round drive punch*
Swivel knife leather tool*
B200 beveler leather tool*
Polymer mallet and punch board*
Leather sheen spray*
½" latigo lace*: Medium brown
AC light socket with cord and 4 watt
 bulb
Drill & 1" hole saw

Two ¼" stencil brushes, ½" brush, 1"
 sponge brush, circle template, cloth
 tape measure, clothes pins, contact
 cement, craft knife and extra #11
 blades, cup, low tack drafting tape,
 pencil, poster board, stencil material,
 fine sandpaper, scissors, straight
 edge ruler, towel

*These products were used: Walnut
Hollow® clock base, clock
movement • The Leather Factory®
goatskin parchment rawhide, lace,
needle, natural leather, round drive
punch, swivel knife, beveler, mallet
and punch board, leather sheen
spray, latigo lace • Minwax® gel
stain • Delta® stencil paint crèmes,
acrylic paint

Note: *Refer to color photos for
application and placement. Let paint,
varnish, and glue dry between
applications.*

KARI LEE

LUMINOSITY OF TIME

FINISHED SIZE: 6½" X 15¾" X 4"

*This oak-stained Arts & Crafts inspired timepiece
was created with some basic woodworking and
leather craft knowledge. Traditional leather
techniques, hand-cut decorative stencils, a rawhide
lampshade, and a tooled clock face made from
natural tanned leather join the wood for a project
with lasting beauty.*

INSTRUCTIONS

Please refer to Luminosity of Time pattern on page 106.

1. To prepare clock, use ruler to determine center of wood base, mark with pencil. Drill 1" hole in center. Use towel with gel stain to stain entire clock.

2. For clock face pattern, use 4½" circle template with pencil to draw circle on poster board. Locate center of circle and draw an additional ½" circle for clock movement. Cut out circles with scissors.

3. To create poster board pattern for lampshade, determine length by using a cloth tape measure to measure around four posts of lamp base and add 1" to measurement. For width of shade, measure height of posts and add ¼" to measurement. *Note: This will account for shrinkage of the rawhide shade.* Total measurements should be approximately 7½" x 17". Along two ends of 17" side, mark position of ⅛" holes needed for assembly, 3/16" from edge, and ¼" from top and bottom edge. Space holes approximately 7/16" apart. Cut out pattern. Place pattern onto punch board, use ⅛" drive punch and mallet to punch stitching holes as marked in pattern.

4. Prepare rawhide by soaking in clean tub of water for about one hour for it to become pliable. Remove rawhide from water, pat dry with towel. Place on cutting surface right side up. Position lampshade pattern along length of rawhide. Use straight edge ruler with craft knife to cut out shade. Secure

luminosity of time

pattern onto rawhide shade with clothes pins, punch holes. Cover with towel until ready to attach.

5. Soak 24" length of rawhide lace in cup of water for approximately 20 minutes or until pliable. Place a two-prong needle onto one lace end. Make an overhand knot on loose end of lace. Wrap cut rawhide shade around four columns of wood base with ends of shade toward back side of clock base and center. Overlap open edge and align holes along bottom edge, place needle through first set of holes along bottom edge from outside. Bring needle back out through second set of holes. Pull lace snug but not tight. The rawhide and lace will naturally shrink as they dry. Continue running stitch working towards top of shade and make an overhand knot to secure lace end. Wait to cut excess lace until shade is completely dry, approximately 24 hours.

6. Transfer stencil patterns onto stencil material, cut pattern with craft knife. Use drafting tape to secure rose stencil to front center of shade. Use stencil brush to brush mix Barn Red and Paprika stencil paint cream, lightly pounce mix into rose area. Using other stencil brush, brush mix Hunter Green and Colonial Green stencil paint

TECHNIQUE:

TO HOLD THE SWIVEL KNIFE, PLACE INDEX FINGER IN FRONT OF FIRST JOINT ON ARCHED YOKE AT TOP OF SWIVEL KNIFE. THE TWO MIDDLE FINGERS AND THUMB ARE TO BE POSITIONED ON SHANK OF TOOL. TO USE TOOL, CENTER BLADE ON SURFACE MAKING SURE NOT TO LEAN TO LEFT OR RIGHT AND WITH TOP OF TOOL LEANING AWAY FROM YOU, PULL TOOL TOWARDS YOU. THE CARVED LINE SHOULD ONLY GO HALF THE DEPTH OF THE LEATHER'S THICKNESS. PRACTICE IS ADVISED.

cream, lightly pounce into squares around rose. Carefully remove stencil and set aside. Position and tape multiple square stencil pattern on one side of shade, stencil design as above. Repeat on other side of shade.

7. Using craft knife, cut clock face from natural leather using poster board pattern as guide. Cut ½" hole in center. Lightly moisten top surface of leather clock face. Position center portion of multiple square stencil pattern on center of leather clock face. Tape in place. Use swivel knife to carve four squares using stencil as a guide.

8. To make carved squares stand out, use smooth beveling tool and mallet to bevel outside edge of swivel knife cut.

TECHNIQUE:

HOLDING TOOL UPRIGHT WITH WIDER END INSERTED INTO CUT LINE, LIGHTLY STRIKE TOOL WITH MALLET, WALKING (MOVING) TOOL SLOWLY ALONG CUT LINE. THE GOAL IS TO KEEP THE BEVELED EDGE AS SMOOTH AS POSSIBLE. PRACTICE IS ADVISED.

9. Use ½" brush to apply smooth, light coat of Antique White over front surface of tooled clock face. Position stencil pattern as before over clock face, aligning with tooled squares. Use stencil brush with Barn Red and Paprika mixture to pounce on squares.

10. Spray light coat of leather sheen to seal and protect all leather surfaces.

11. Use contact cement to adhere clock face onto wood base. For additional leather accent in detailed cut channel in wood around face of clock, cut a length of latigo lace to fit, secure with contact cement.

12. Attach clock movement and hands following directions on back of packaging. Insert light socket and bulb into hole of lamp base.

MATERIALS

Wooden doll furniture cupboard*
Clock movement with hands for ¾"
    surface*
Large wood wheel, small wood wheel,
    wood knob
Acrylic Paint*:
    Light Ivory
    Eucalyptus
    Moss Green
    Forest Green
    Wisteria
    Dusty Plum
Mediums*:
    All-purpose sealer
    Satin interior varnish
    Clear glaze base
    Fine crackle: #1 and #2
    Texture builder
Stencils and tools*: Delicate vines
    frames and accents
    Harlequin
    Stencil adhesive
    Stencil sponges
Thick craft glue*
Brushes: #1 liner, #16 flat, 1" flat

Drill with ⅜" bit, glass knobs, masking
    tape, palette, paper towels, pencil,
    sanding sponge block, small spatula

*These products were used: Walnut
    Hollow® cupboard, clock movement
    with hands • Delta® paint, mediums,
    stencils, and tools • Sobo® glue

Note: *Refer to color photos for
application and placement. Let paint,
mediums, varnish, and glue dry
between applications.*

CHERYL BALL—COURTESY OF DELTA TECHNICAL COATINGS
STENCILED CUPBOARD

FINISHED SIZE: 10¼" X 10¾" X 4⅞"

*Dimension can add so much. Using a variety
of stencils is an easy way to create a great
look. Combine everything with Texture
Builder and a crackle finish, and you have a
fabulous project.*

INSTRUCTIONS

1. Remove knobs from cupboard doors. Use 1"
flat brush to apply one coat of sealer to the
entire cupboard. Sand lightly with sanding
sponge block when dry.

2. To basecoat cupboard, use 1" flat brush to
apply two coats of Light Ivory.

3. To stencil background, tape off 3" x 3" row
of harlequins on stencil. Spray stencil
adhesive to back of stencil following label
instructions. Center stencil design on door
of cupboard, press to secure. Tap flat end of
sponge into Moss Green, tap excess off on
palette. Pounce sponge into stencil, filling in
areas. Carefully remove stencil and
reposition on other door. Continue
stenciling, taping off 2" x 3" section for sides
and an 8" x 2" section for top.

4. Use the liner brush with Wisteria to paint a
thin line around each stenciled section.

5. To apply wash to remaining sections of
cupboard, use 1" flat brush with Eucalyptus
thinned with water, approximately 1 to 1.

6. To shade next to each stenciled section, use
#16 flat brush to float with Eucalyptus
Green.

7. To apply textured stencil design, place
Texture Builder onto palette, mix thoroughly
with small amount of Light Ivory. Cut apart
designs of vine stencil, place into position
on cupboard. Remove, spray adhesive to
backs, reposition, press to secure. Use
masking tape to mask off any areas or edges
of stencil as needed. Scoop up a small
amount of the mixture with small spatula
and lightly "frost" the stencil, leaving a thin
even coating. Carefully remove stencil.
Continue with remaining designs. Wash
stencils with water when finished.

stenciled cupboard

8. To paint design, make smaller sponges by cutting sponges in half lengthwise and then in half again, creating a sponge for each color to be applied. Securely reposition stencils over dried designs. Use small sponge to pounce following colors: Wisteria for flowers; Dusty Plum to shade flower centers, berries; Eucalyptus for leaves; Forest Green to shade leaves.

9. Use drill with bit to make hole for clock in center of left door. Use pencil to lightly draw circle for numbers about 1½" from drilled hole. Lightly draw numbers.

10. Use #1 liner brush to paint numbers Forest Green. Carefully erase any pencil lines.

11. Use #1 liner with Wisteria to apply two coats to centers of knobs and clock hands.

12. To paint wheels and knob, use #16 flat to basecoat with the following colors. Large wheel: basecoat Forest Green, use #1 liner for stripes of Moss Green. Small wheel: basecoat Wisteria, use #1 liner to add vines and leaves of Forest Green, add dot berries

of Dusty Plum and Light Ivory. Knob: basecoat Eucalyptus.

13. To crackle entire cupboard, use 1" flat brush to apply two even coats of Step #1 Fine Crackle following label instructions. Apply one even coat of Step #2 Fine Crackle over everything and let dry overnight for cracks to appear.

14. To antique, mix Clear Glaze Base and Forest Green on palette. Working in small sections, use #1 flat brush to apply one coat of mixture, pushing paint into cracks. Immediately wipe off excess with soft paper towel. Continue until complete. For added depth, bunch up one paper towel, tap into mixture, and softly pounce color around top and front edges of cupboard.

15. Use #1 flat brush to apply one coat of Satin Varnish to all pieces. Glue wheels and knob to top, attach glass knobs, and attach clock movement and hands following directions on back of packaging.

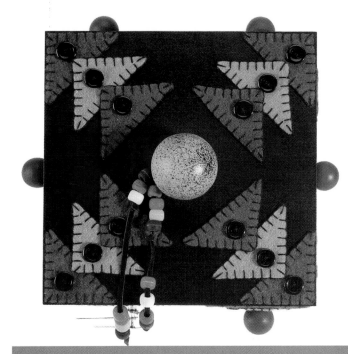

MATERIALS

Wood box with hinged lid and ball
   feet*
Clock movement for ⅜" surface*
1⅜" clock hands*
Five ¾" ball knobs
Felt*: ⅛ yard Cranberry
   9" x 12" sheets: Denim, Antique
   Gold, Sandstone
Black embroidery floss
Iron-on backing, 3½" square
Freezer paper (optional)
Twelve ⁷⁄₁₆" black buttons
24" length ⅛" wide black leather lace
Fifteen 9 x 6 mm barrel pony beads*
Acrylic paint*:
   Lamp Black
   Navy Blue
   Khaki Tan
   White Wash
Black spray paint
Spray matte sealer/finisher*
Flat paint brushes: 1, ¼"
Drill with ⅜" bit
Fabric glue*

Air-soluble pen, embroidery needle,
   fine sandpaper, iron, old toothbrush,
   paper towels, pencil, ruler, scissors,
   two small paper cups, tack cloth

* These products were used: Walnut
   Hollow® box, knobs, clock
   movements • Deco Art® paint,
   sealer • Kunin Rainbow™ felt •
   Beacon Fabri-Tac™ adhesive • The
   Beadery® beads

Note: *Refer to color photo for
application and placement. Let paint,
varnish, and glue dry between
applications.*

CHRIS MALONE
FOLK ART CLOCK BOX

FINISHED SIZE: 6¼" X 7¾" X 6¼"

*Turn a plain wood box into a folk-art décor
accent by adding felt, leather, and bead
embellishments. Hand stitching adds the
perfect finishing touch.*

INSTRUCTIONS

Please refer to Folk Art Clock Box pattern on page 110.

1. Sand box lightly and wipe with tack cloth.

2. To basecoat box, use 1" brush to paint outside of box Black. Paint ball feet and top knob Khaki Tan.

3. To match blue felt, mix a few drops of White Wash into Navy Blue in small paper cup. Use 1" brush to paint ¾" ball knobs.

4. To spatter box, mix water and Black paint (1 to 1) in small paper cup. Dip toothbrush into mixture and blot excess on paper towel. Holding toothbrush over box, run thumb across bristles to spatter paint.

5. Spray entire box, inside and out, with two light coats of sealer/finisher.

6. Use patterns to trace 10 squares, 5 hearts, and 12 triangles on dull side of freezer paper, leaving ½" between each shape. Cut out ¼" from lines leaving patterns uncut in groups: two sets of squares, three sets of triangles, and five hearts.

7. Place shiny side of wax paper on felt and press with iron for three seconds to adhere to felt in the following way: 5 squares each on Antique Gold and Denim; 4 triangles each on Antique Gold, Denim, and Cranberry; 5 hearts on Cranberry. Cut along traced lines through paper and felt.

8. Use two strands of black embroidery floss for all stitching. Blanket stitch around each square and each triangle. Blanket stitch one heart to center of each Denim square. With floss, sew a black button near top point of each triangle.

9. To make clock face, follow manufacturer's directions to apply iron-on backing to one side of Sandstone felt. Cut 1 clock face. Use air-soluble pen to transfer clock markings to edge of clock face. Blanket stitch around edge of face, making five-minute stitches twice as long as other stitches. Spray paint

clock hands until completely covered with Black.

10. Drill hole through box front 1⅞" from edge, centered vertically. Cut hole in center of clock face large enough for shank of clock. Adhere face to box using fabric glue, matching holes. Attach clock movement and hands following directions on back of packaging.

11. Cut a 2½" x 21¼" strip of Cranberry felt. Blanket stitch around edges. Apply fabric glue to wrong side of Cranberry strip, starting at right end and working with ⅓ of strip at a time. Glue does not need to cover entire width of strip, but should be close to edge. Press end to corner edge of left side of box, centering vertically. Continue around box, being careful not to stretch felt. Strip should end in front, near clock face.

12. Glue small ball knobs to center of Antique Gold squares. Glue square to center of Cranberry strip on front of clock. Continue gluing squares on strip, alternating Antique Gold squares and Denim squares and having three squares on each side of box.

13. Glue a Cranberry triangle to each corner of box lid. Place one Antique Gold triangle, then one Denim triangle on each corner, overlapping slightly. Glue triangles in place.

14. Wrap suede lace around lid knob twice and tie knot. Thread three beads on each lace and tie a knot close to beads. Thread four beads on each lace. Tie a knot 1½" below beads. Trim lace ends below knots.

folk art clock box

MATERIALS

Wooden square clock*
Clock movement for ¾" surface*
Black clock hands*
Antique adhesive clock face*
Acrylic paint*:
  Antique White
  Burnt Umber
  Dark Foliage Green
  Empire Gold
  Georgia Clay
  Golden Brown
  Mocha Brown
  Tompte Red
  Wedgwood Green
  White
Mediums*:
  Instant Age Varnish
  Clear Glaze Base
Brushes*: #3 and #6 rounds
  #4 shader
  #1 liner
  ¾" wash
Black Identipen*

#2 pencil with eraser, fine grit
  sandpaper, foam plate, graphite
  paper, masking tape, paper towels,
  tack cloth, toothpick, tracing paper

*These products were used: Walnut
  Hollow® square clock, clock
  movement, black clock hands,
  adhesive clock face • Delta® paints,
  mediums • Loew-Cornell® brushes •
  Sakura® black pen

Note: Refer to color photos for
application and placement. Let paint,
varnish, and glue dry between
applications.

VICKI SCHREINER
FOUR SEASONS

FINISHED SIZE: 12" X 12" X ¾"

*Create a beautiful hand-painted clock
celebrating each season of the year. Easy
techniques are used to give it an antiqued look.*

INSTRUCTIONS

Please refer to Four Seasons pattern on pages 96 and 97.

1. To prepare surface, lightly sand square clock, remove dust with tack cloth.

2. Mix equal parts Glaze Base and Dark Foliage Green on foam plate. Use ¾" wash brush to apply one coat of mixture to outside beveled edge of clock. Apply two coats Antique White to front and back.

3. Trace pattern onto tracing paper using pen. Tape pattern to clock, slip graphite paper between pattern and clock, and trace pattern with pencil. Do not transfer stippled dots, which are for shading reference.
   Note: To paint pattern use appropriate size brush to fit area being painted.

4. Undercoat as follows:
   Winter—Undercoat leaves Wedgwood Green and berries Tompte Red.
   Spring—Undercoat leaves Wedgwood Green and flowers Empire Gold.
   Summer—Undercoat leaves, stems, strawberry caps Wedgwood Green, flower petals

White, flower centers Empire Gold, and strawberries Tompte Red.
   Fall—Undercoat leaves Empire Gold, acorns Mocha Brown, acorn caps Golden Brown, and border stripe Mocha Brown.

5. Transfer pattern details using graphite paper.

6. Mix equal parts Glaze Base with each color acrylic paint on foam plate. Working on small areas at a time, shade as follows: Load brush with small amount of paint, stroke on palette to remove some of paint. Dab paint in area to be shaded. Quickly dry brush on paper towel. Pat dry brush onto applied paint to blend and soften. Repeat to darken.
   Winter—Shade leaves Dark Foliage Green and berries Burnt Umber.
   Spring—Shade leaves Dark Foliage Green and flowers Georgia Clay.
   Summer—shade leaves, stems, and strawberry caps Dark Foliage Green. Shade

four seasons

flower petals, flower centers, and strawberries Burnt Umber.

Fall—shade top of left leaf Dark Foliage Green and bottom of left leaf Georgia Clay. Shade top of right leaf Dark Foliage Green and bottom of right leaf Tompte Red. Shade top of middle leaf Georgia Clay and shade bottom of middle leaf Tompte Red. Shade acorns and acorn caps Burnt Umber. On all designs, shade again along all areas that overlap each other or areas requiring greater depth using Burnt Umber. Also, shade areas on border stripe with Burnt Umber.

7. Mix equal parts Glaze Base with White on foam plate for all highlighting steps. Refer to highlighting diagram. Pounce highlights as follows: Load brush with small amount of paint. Stroke brush on paper towel until dry (there will be enough paint residue left in bristles to add soft color). Holding brush in upright position, pounce area to be highlighted. Repeat to lighten

Winter—Lightly highlight center of each berry.

Spring—Highlight down center of each flower pod.

Summer—Highlight along right side of each strawberry.

Fall—Highlight along right side of each acorn and across center of each acorn cap.

Apply additional highlights as follows: Load brush with small amount of paint. Stroke on palette to remove some of paint. Stroke paint in area to be shaded. Quickly dry brush on paper towel. Pat dry brush onto applied paint to blend and soften.

Winter—Highlight leaves.

Spring—Highlight leaves and flower petals.

Summer—Highlight leaves and strawberry caps.

8. To finish details, outline designs using fine tip of black pen. Do not outline border stripe. Also, using fine tip as follows:

Winter—Darkly fill in dot on each berry.

Summer—Darkly fill in seeds on each strawberry, add several random scattered dots around each flower center. Outline curly vines on winter and summer designs using wide tip.

9. Use #1 liner brush with Golden Brown to paint all lettering.

10. Add other details as follows:

Winter—Add small comma stroke to right side of each berry with White. Using toothpick, add a tiny dot to each berry dot with White.

Spring—Using liner brush, add three small stamen to inside of each flower with White. Using toothpick, add a small dot to top of each stamen with Georgia Clay.

Summer—Using liner brush, add a small highlight line down right side of each berry with White, add small comma stroke to right side of each flower center with White, add small mark to center of each strawberry seed with Empire Gold.

11. To antique and varnish clock at the same time, use ¾" wash brush to apply one coat varnish to front and back of clock.

12. To adhere clock face, remove backing and press in place.

13. Attach clock movement and hands following directions on back of packaging.

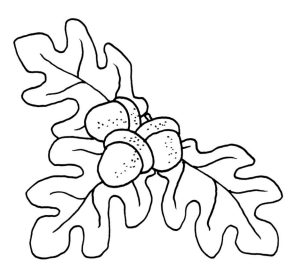

Highlighting Diagrams

MATERIALS

Mini bezel clock movement*
Beads*:
  Luster Mix #162412
  Trans. Luster Mix #B2002
  11/0 Seed Beads Met. Silver #CZ107
72" 16 gauge silver wire*
78" 28 gauge silver wire*
⅛" pattern WireMesh™*

Black felt tip marker, compass,
  embroidery scissors, needle-nose
  pliers, ruler, scrap paper, wire cutters

*These products were used: Walnut
  Hollow® bezel clock movement •
  AMACO® wire, wire mesh • Crafts
  Etc!™ beads

Note: *Refer to color photos for
placement.*

KOREN RUSSELL
RING OF JEWELS

FINISHED SIZE: 6¼" X 3½" X 3¼"

The glass beads shine like jewels around the rim of this desk clock. You can choose to buy new beads for this project or use leftover beads from previous projects.

INSTRUCTIONS

1. To create clock mesh piece, draw 3"circle on scrap paper with compass. Cut circle with scissors, place pattern on top of mesh, cut mesh circle.

2. To create clock frame, begin by cutting a 17" piece of 16 gauge wire. Use black pen to place mark on wire 3" from one end. Place another mark 9½" from first mark. At 3" mark, bend wire at 90-degree angle to form "L" to create stem.

3. Hold onto stem, curve next 9½" of wire up and around to the left then down and round to the right to form 3" circle (9½" mark should sit right behind stem). The remaining wire to right of 9½" mark will fall off to right of stem. It will look like a lollipop or bubble wand. Check wire circle against mesh circle for size. The wire circle must be slightly smaller, or exact size, as mesh.

4. Bend remaining wire up and around stem three times. Trim wire to end just behind stem. Use pliers to squeeze these three wraps together.

5. Cut 48" piece of 28 gauge wire, fold in half. Turn stem to top with front side of wire circle facing forward (trimmed wire from wraps will be in back). Place mesh circle behind wire, hold two pieces together.

6. At 3 o'clock position, thread one end of 28 gauge wire through mesh next to circle wire and through a full diamond in mesh. Pull wire until reaching fold in wire. Wrap one end of wire around wire circle and through mesh in same spot. Repeat.
Note: *Always pull wire snug but not so tight it breaks through mesh.*

7. Pick up wire end that is on top of mesh to add beads clockwise around circle, leaving second section of wire alone for now.

8. To sew circle wire and mesh together with a simple stitch using beaded wire, thread a few beads onto wire, adding at least one small silver bead before and after a glass bead.

ring of jewels

Bring wire around wire circle and to back, thread through mesh, and pull wire tight. Continue sewing with a line of beads, varying the amount, color and size of beads. Go around the wire circle and mesh twice. Leave a ½" tail and trim off excess.

9. Pick up second section of wire and continue beading clockwise. This time fill in back of clock. Sew lines of beads over or under previous stitches, filling in around circle. When close to completing second row of beading, bend ½" tail from first wire against wire circle. While completing second row, treat tail and wire circle as one so that beading wire holds tail securely against wire circle. To end wire, wrap beading wire around wire circle and through mesh twice, leave a ½" tail, and trim off excess.

   Note: To keep all wires from starting and ending at same point, end second wire short of completing second row or after starting third row.

10. Cut a new beading wire, 30" long, attach to left of where second wire ended. Wrap one end around wire circle and through mesh twice. Leave a ½" tail and trim excess. Bend tail from this wire and tail from end of second wire to the right against wire circle. Treat tails same as wire circle. Continue beading for a third row. The purpose of this row is to make sure back looks nice and to fill in any open areas on front of clock. To end third wire, wrap it around wire circle and through mesh three times. Leave a ½" tail, trim off excess, push tail in amongst beads to hide.

11. Hold stem wire 2" above wraps. Bend stem wire down to the right, into a circle about ⅜" wide. There should be ½" gap between wraps and start of circle. Start to bend another circle right behind first circle. When half of circle is formed, cut excess wire. The end of second circle should end halfway down on the right side of first circle.

12. Place mini bezel clock movement face down. Center beaded circle face down over top. Trace around black circle on back of mini bezel onto mesh using marker. Cut mesh along line. Enlarge hole a bit at a time until mini bezel fits into hole. Press mini bezel gently into hole.

13. To create stand, cut one 50" piece of 16 gauge wire, bending wire at a 45-degree angle (L shape) 3" from one end. This first 3" is stem. Using same technique as above, hold onto stem, curve long length of wire up and around to the left then down and round to the right, into a 3½" circle. The remaining wire will lie on top of stem wire. Continue to form circles until there are three 3½" circles. The remaining wire will fall off to the right of stem and on top of it.

14. Wrap 3" stem up and around circles three times to hold together. Trim off stem wire to end under circles. Use pliers to squeeze three wraps together.

15. Bend remaining long length of wire back against wraps and straight up, forming an L with wraps. 7" from this bend fold wire back down like a hair pin, 7" from top fold, bend wire to the right at a 90 degree angle, forming another L.

16. Visually divide the three circles into thirds, starting with wraps around circles. Place last bend in wire under wire circles ⅓ of way around circle, to the right, of wraps. Wrap remaining wire up and around wire circles three times. Trim off excess wire under circles. Use pliers to squeeze three wraps together, creating a triangle towering above circle base.

17. Cut 5" piece of 16 gauge wire. Place center of wire under wire circles ⅓ of the distance around circle, to the right, of last wraps. Wrap wire around circles three times, trimming off excess wire under circles. Use pliers to squeeze three wraps together.

18. Squeeze two wires at top of triangle together. Curve top 2" of the stand down around finger. Using pliers, bend tip up into a hook.

MATERIALS

Two 24" scalloped shelves*
11" provincial shelf*
Square frame*
Large regulator clock*
Large pendulum clock movement with hands*
PutAway Wardrobe*
Satin acrylic sealer/finisher*
Satin acrylic enamel paint*:
  2 cans/bottles Soft White
  2 cans/bottles Light Willow
  Buttercream
Acrylic paint*: Emperors Gold Metallic
Bravissimo! Papers* 8½" x 11" sheets:
  Silver
  Garnet Swirl
  Two Opulent
Cardstock* 8½" x 11" sheet:
  Two Light Sage
Craft Punches*:
  Super Jumbo—Quilt Diamond 60°, Circle
  Super Giant—Sun, Allegro, Oval
  Large—Square, Oval, Circle
  Small—Quasar
3 cup hooks
5 yards chain
2 angle brackets
Three 8" dowels
Two 1" x 4" x 4' wood boards

4 sponge brushes, finishing nails, foam plate, hammer, screwdriver, and wood screws

*These products were used: Walnut Hollow® shelves, frame, wardrobe, clock, pendulum movement • DecoArt™ sealer/finisher, enamel paint, acrylic paint • Emagination Crafts, Inc. paper, punches • DMD® cardstock

Note: *Refer to color photos for application and placement. Let paint and varnish dry between applications.*

VIVIAN PERITTS
GRANDFATHER CLOCK

FINISHED SIZE: 17¾" X 69½" X 7⅛"

Using wood, paint, paper, punches, and your imagination, you can create your own grandfather clock, complete with chimes.

INSTRUCTIONS

Please refer to Grandfather Clock pattern on page 110.

1. Paint all wood pieces.
   Note: *It is recommended that you paint each individual piece with a base coat of White paint and at least 2 coats of your choice of paint color.*

2. On large flat surface, lay 1" x 4" x 4' boards side by side, with narrow edge up. Position wardrobe at one end so ends of boards are against top of wardrobe. At opposite end, place clock face between boards. Arrange so indented edge of clock face is flush with top of boards and top edge of boards is flush with top edge of clock face. Using finishing nails and hammer, secure in place.

3. Position square frame on top of boards and behind top of wardrobe. Using finishing nails and hammer, secure in place.

4. Position scalloped shelf on one side of clock face, turning shelf so that scalloped edge is flush with narrow edge of 1" x 4" x 4' board and even with top edge of board. Using finishing nails and hammer, secure in place. Repeat for other shelf.

5. Position provincial shelf on top of, and immediately behind, clock face so that shelf is upside down and bottom of shelf faces out. Using finishing nails, attach to ends to 1" x 4" x 4' boards.

6. Attach angle brackets to bottom ends of 1" x 4" x 4' boards, flush with bottom of board and positioned so they will connect boards to top of wardrobe. Securely attach brackets to boards and to wardrobe with screws.

7. Attach cup hooks into back of clock face and hang chains with dowels, adjusting length of chain to varying lengths.

8. Attach pendulum movement and hands following directions on back of packaging.

9. Following Design Legend for Punches and Papers, punch out shapes.

Design Legend

Punches:

1—Quilt Diamond
2—Sun
3—Allegro
4—Quasar
5—Circle (super jumbo)
6—Circle (jumbo)
7—Oval (super jumbo)
8—Oval (jumbo)
9—Square

Papers:

A—Opulent
B—Silver
C—Garnet Swirl
D—Light Sage

Punch out the following:

10 of A-1
1 of A-5
4 of A-6
2 of B-2
1 of B-3
28 of B-4
4 of B-5
4 of C-3
1 of C-6
18 of C-7
11 of C-8
4 of D-3
5 of D-6
11 of D-8
12 of D-9

10. Referring to Figure A on page 110, apply designs by brushing a small amount of sealer/finisher on area and position shape, making sure all edges are securely in place. Brush each shape again with sealer/finisher. Finished design should appear to be embedded in painted surface.
Note: Sealer/finisher will appear white, but will dry clear.

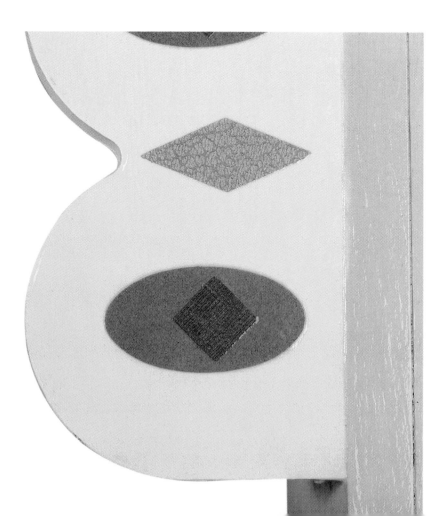

grandfather clock

MATERIALS

Wood clock circle*
Clock movement and hands for ¾"
   surface*
Polymer clay*:
   Black
   (2) White
   Ultra Blue
   Magenta
   Red
   Yellow
   Green
   Orange
   Copper
   Gold
   Violet
Marking ruler*
Cutting blade*
Glue*

Acrylic rod, bamboo skewer, pasta
   machine

* These products were used: Walnut
   Hollow® clock, clock movement •
   Kato Polyclay® clay • Marxit Kato®
   marking ruler • Nublade Kato®
   cutting blade • Sobo® glue

DONNA KATO
FUNKY FACE

FINISHED SIZE: 4½" ROUND

Create a fun and funky face with polymer clay. The entire clock face is baked on the wooden clock to complete the curing process!

GENERAL INFORMATION

Polymer clay must be conditioned prior to use. Method 1: Simply cut block into chunks, knead each chunk until soft and pliable, mix chunks together. Method 2: Cut ¼" thick slices from blocks. Roll each slice through the thickest setting of the pasta machine. Finish by folding and rolling slices through until sheet is soft and pliable. Colors may be mixed to create custom palettes.

COLOR MIXES

Lime Green–Mix small bits of Green into Yellow until desired color is achieved. A small amount of this accent color is needed.
Copper Gold–Mix equal parts (⅛ package) Copper and Gold.

Note: Refer to color photos for application and placement.

INSTRUCTIONS

1. To make clay to cover wooden clock edge, cut strip of black clay width of edge and roll through thickest setting of pasta machine. Apply glue only to edge of clock. Press clay strip to edge, working around, trimming end of strip to form a butt joint. Smooth edges together with fingers, then gently coax clay down to bottom of clock base. Set aside.

2. To make Striped Slab Cane, roll a sheet of Black and a sheet of White (half package of

funky face

each) each through thickest setting of pasta machine. Place one sheet atop other and, using Nublade, trim four sides. Through same setting of pasta machine, roll two-color slab through machine again. This will create thin stripes. Cut sheet in half and place one half atop other. Repeat two more times to make a striped slab.

3. To make clay for edges, lay Marxit ruler across either black or white side of slab and gently press to transfer marks. Use Nublade cutter to cut several slices. Roll each slice through thickest setting of pasta machine. Reset machine to next thinner setting and roll through again. Continue resetting and rolling each slice until you have rolled through a medium-thin to thin setting. Trim one end of the thin, long strip. These striped strips will be used to create banding along clock face edge.

   Note: The direction the clay is rolled through the pasta machine is important. Slices should be rolled through to elongate them, not make stripes wider.

4. To attach stripes, begin by positioning striped strip along lower edge, trim bottom with blade. Press sides of slice to clay-covered edge so that edges point directly at center hole. Using fingers, gently press the remaining clay from bottom edge toward upper edge. Use Nublade to trim excess clay away. Continue until edge is covered, using acrylic rod to smooth slices, joining any seams.

   Note: As upper edge is a smaller diameter than lower edge, it is necessary to line up lower edge, then ease upper edge into place.

5. To cover clock face, cut a circle large enough to fit the face from sheet of clay. Lightly coat wooden face with glue, and carefully press cut circle to clock face. Press out any air pockets. Remove the clay from the center hole of the clock. Set aside.

6. To make cheeks, use White and Magenta (¼ package of each), and make a Skinner Blend (see next page). Once sheet is made, fold sheet in half again as if to continue to blend sheet. Roll folded sheet through pasta machine, placing Magenta edge on rollers. You now have a long, thin, Skinner Blended strip. Reset pasta machine to a medium-thin setting and roll clay through, feeding Magenta edge through again. Trim the Magenta edge and the White edge. From the Magenta edge, roll up tightly. Trim one edge

to make a large shaded bull's-eye with Magenta in center and White on outer edge. Cut two thin slices, lightly position them at 3 and 9 o'clock. Reposition, if necessary. Once satisfied with their position, press them to clay face. Reduce bull's-eye to half its original diameter by gently pressing sides of cane and rolling to smooth. Let cane rest for later use.

7. To make eyelids, mix ¼ package of Gold and ¼ package of Copper. Skinner Blend this mixture to black. Repeat instructions for cheeks to make large shaded bull's-eye with Copper/Gold center and black on outer edge. Cut one thin slice from cane. Cut this slice in half. Position and press eyelids to face.

8. To make lips, Skinner Blend White to Violet (¼ package each). Roll bull's-eye so that Violet is in center and White on outside of cane. Working against your work surface, reshape this cane to shape of upper and lower lips. Cut one slice and press to face to make lower lip. Cut another slice and press over lower lip to make upper lip.

9. From reduced cheek cane, cut two slices and place in position below cheeks.

10. For face details, roll thin tapering Black "snakes"—two for eyes, one for nose and one for lips. Place in position. Roll two red balls. Place one each at corners of lip lines. Flatten and pierce centers with bamboo skewer. Roll two small orange balls, drop one ball onto each flattened red ball and gently tamp with fingers. For eyebrows, cut two thin pieces of striped cane used for edges. Position and press them to face.

11. To designate hours on clock face, roll four small Black balls. Press them to the 12, 3, 6 and 9 o'clock positions on clock face. Press center of each ball with bamboo skewer. Mix Lime Green. Roll four small balls, drop one in the center of each flattened Black ball and gently tamp tops.

12. For clock face borders, roll a thin snake of Ultra Blue and wrap around inner edge. Roll a thin snake of black and wrap around outer edge.

13. Use corner of blade to trim center hole out of clock.

14. Bake at 275 degrees F for 45 minutes. If, once cured, there are any air pockets between clay and wood, press them flat with an oven mitt until the piece is cooled.

Note: You may leave clock as it is or lightly sand surface with 400 grit wet/dry sandpaper to clean face of any lint or contaminating bits of clay.

15. Attach clock movement and hands following directions on back of packaging.

SKINNER BLEND

Preparation: Roll two colors into sheets of the same thickness.

1. Stack one color on top of the other and cut a right angle (90°) triangle.

2. Separate the two sheets and join together along the diagonal edges, offsetting the colors slightly in order to have pure color areas.

3. Fold the two-color sheet in half. Roll through pasta machine on the thickest (⅛") setting. Fold and roll through again.

4. Repeat until colors are graduated. Be sure to fold the same way each time.

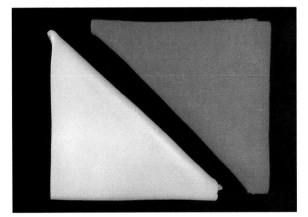
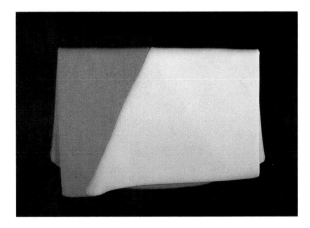

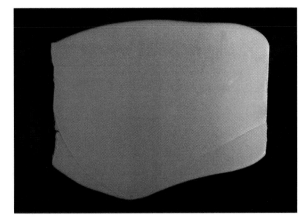

Designers

CINDY GORDER

Cindy Gorder has been a professional graphic artist for more than 25 years, working in all areas of designing and producing commercially printed materials. In addition she designs craft projects for publication, working mainly with fabrics, beads, polymer clay, colored pencils and paper. She also enjoys wood carving, rubber stamping, decoupage, and wire crafts, and likes to combine surfaces and techniques for unique creations.

CHERYL BALL

Cheryl Ball is the design studio manager for Delta Technical Coatings of Whittier, California, where she creates projects for magazines, television shows, trade shows, projects for packaging, and much more. Her designs have appeared in several magazines through the years and have been featured on the "Carol Duvall Show" several times. Ball also worked for Duncan Enterprises of Fresno, California, as one of their in-house designers. For six years she was responsible for a weekly segment on kids' crafts for "Aleene's Creative Living" television show. She also managed a craft and gift store for 15 years.

CINDY GROOM-HARRY

Cindy Groom-Harry is CEO and head designer of Craft Marketing Connections Inc. of Ireton, Iowa. She and her design/marketing team have created more than 4,000 published designs and have written more than 500 magazine articles for *Better Homes & Gardens, Woman's Day, Parents Magazine, Good Housekeeping, McCall's, Simplicity*, and nearly every craft magazine. She has appeared on more than 100 television shows and starred in two dozen videos. She and her staff have authored 40 how-to books and co-authored 26 more.

PHYLLIS M. DOBBS

Phyllis M. Dobbs has been designing needlework professionally for 18 years. She has always loved needlework and was taught various needlework techniques at an early age by her mother and aunt. She started designing counted cross stitch, then branched into various other forms of needlework, including quilt design. She graduated from the University of Alabama with a degree in interior design and applies the principles learned there to her designing. Phyllis self-published cross stitch for five years, then switched to free-lance designing for publications and manufacturers. She just released a contemporary quilt book, *Dimensional Quilts,* published by Krause Publications of Iola, Wisconsin.

PRISCILLA S. HAUSER

As founder of the Society of Decorative Painters, Priscilla S. Hauser is affectionately dubbed the "First Lady of Decorative Painting." From her beginning efforts as a tole painter in the early 1960s, she has become a world-renowned teacher, author, and decorative painting's ambassador to the world. She teaches extensively throughout the United States and at her "Studio by the Sea" in Panama City Beach, Florida. Hauser shares her enthusiasm for decorative painting by illustrating her techniques in books, magazine articles, videos, and on television. The latest of many prestigious awards bestowed upon Priscilla include the Hobby Industries of America Hall of Fame Award and the Priscilla Hauser Award for Business & Industry.

LYNNE FARRIS

Lynne Farris brings a lifetime of experience in fabric arts to the world of crafts and do-it-yourself home décor. Her designs are often featured in leading craft magazines, and she is a frequent guest on HGTV. Lynne works as a creative consultant to several leading manufacturers. She is the owner of Lynne Farris Gallery in Atlanta, Georgia, where many of her works are on display.

PAM HAWKINS

Inspired by her always creative mom, Loretta, and Priscilla Hauser, Pam Hawkins' first love has been decorative painting for over 15 years. Having taught a variety of media for 10 years, Pam relocated from Southern California to Wisconsin to become the education, media and design manager for Walnut Hollow of Dodgeville, Wisconsin. A former semi-truck driver, she shares her creative time with her two spoiled poodles, Maggie and Sissy.

DONNA KATO

Donna Kato has been a polymer clay artist for many years, writing books on the subject, as well as making many television appearances demonstrating different clay techniques. She has developed her own line of polymer clay, Kato Polyclay®, with all of the properties that she considers most important to working with this medium.

KARI LEE

Kari Lee has been working and designing in the craft industry for 20 years. She is an experienced designer with many products, but her primary interest for the last eight years has been creating with and marketing leather. Research and new product development is a significant part of her job. She has designed numerous kits and project ideas for The Leather Factory as well as authored many projects featured in trade and consumer magazines and is a contributing designer for books. She is author of *Gorgeous Leather* (Lark Publishing) and is currently working on another leather book for Krause Publications of Iola, Wisconsin. She has appeared on several craft television shows and teaches at trade show events.

CHRIS MALONE

A member of the Society of Craft Designers, Chris Malone has had hundreds of designs published in magazines and books. She loves creating crafts with many different mediums and techniques, but has a special fondness for working with felt and fabric. She finds it particularly satisfying to design a project that is traditionally non-fabric/sewing and make it with fabric, felt, and floss.

VIVIAN PERITTS

Vivian Peritts is a well-known designer, crafter, and author. After earning a degree in art education from the University of South Carolina, she worked for 12 years as an art instructor in the public schools of Cobb County, Georgia. She was the originator and designer of "The Patch Factory," which featured more than 100 original designs for soft-sculpture characters and wall hangings, many of which became McCall's patterns. Her designs have appeared in numerous national publications, including *McCall's*, *Woman's Day*, *Family Circle*, and *Better Homes and Gardens Wearable Crafts*. She has authored 25 pattern books for *McCall's Creates*, taught many workshops at national trade shows, and been a frequent guest on several national cable television shows.

KOREN RUSSELL

Koren Russell is a jack-of-all-trades in crafting and home décor. Skilled in woodworking, paper crafts, painting, sewing, metal work, and basketry, she has designed more than 65 projects for publications and is currently working on two craft books. She dabbles in a variety of mediums to create home décor projects and enjoys using old mediums in new ways. Her goal is to teach and inspire others to discover their abilities and ways to express themselves.

VICKI SCHREINER

Vicki Schreiner's areas of expertise include woodburning, decorative painting, and line art design for scrapbooking, counted cross stitch, stencils, and more. Her experience in the craft industry includes being co-chair of the Society of Craft Designers Seminar 2001 and Delta Associate Designer (2000 to present). She demonstrates products on television, engages in free-lance design for magazine publications, and writes instructional books on woodburning and decorative painting. Vicki has also taught technique classes and demonstrates at both the Association of Crafts & Creative Industries and Hobby Industry Association conventions (1996 to present).

CAROLYN STEARNS

Carolyn Stearns has loved arts and crafts as long as she can remember; craft time at summer camp was better them swimming! Even as family and children took priority and her arts and crafts took a back seat, she always managed to make Christmas gifts for family members each year. When her children grew up, she was able to go back to her first love—arts and crafts. She is most well known for her whimsical painting style. Her designs usually bring a smile to the faces of people viewing them, and that is what she lives for!

CHRIS WALLACE

A decorative painter by heart for 29 years, Chris works as the director of marketing for Walnut Hollow in Dodgeville, Wisconsin. With appearances on many television craft shows and writing articles and columns for painting and craft magazines, Chris is able to share her love of painting, especially stroke work and folk art. She is very involved in the craft industry and various associations, and enjoys the opportunities of sharing the importance of educational experiences and working with so many different people from around the world.

Winter turns to

turns to

FOUR
SEASONS

Fall

turns to

Spring turns to Summer

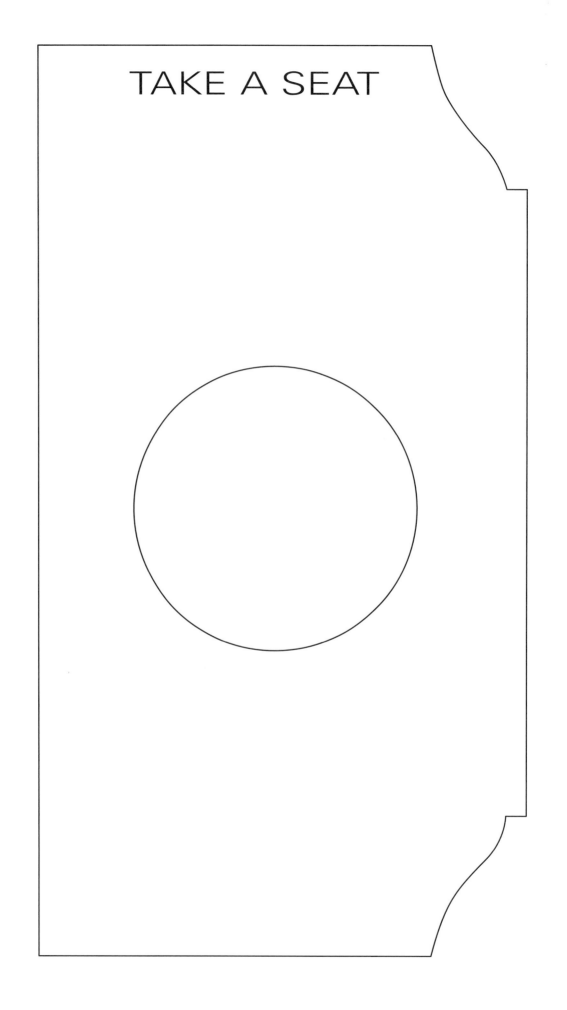

TAKE A SEAT

FRESH FLOWERS CORNER SHELF

Left Side

Right Side

ART DECO

ART DECO

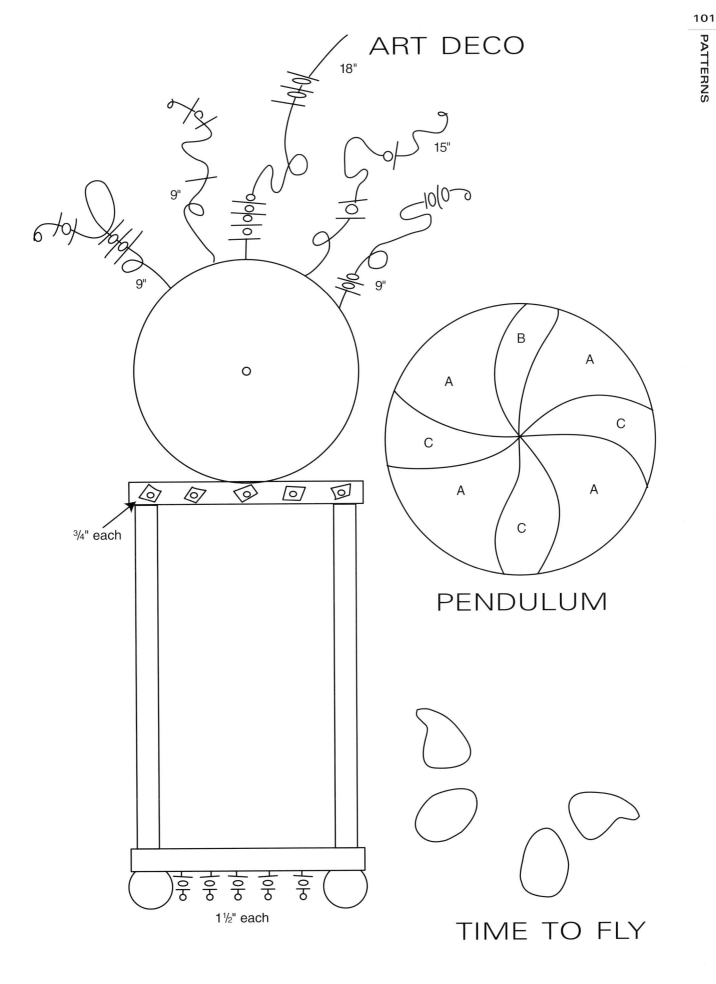

18"

15"

9"

9"

6

9"

9"

¾" each

1½" each

PENDULUM

TIME TO FLY

SITTING PRETTY

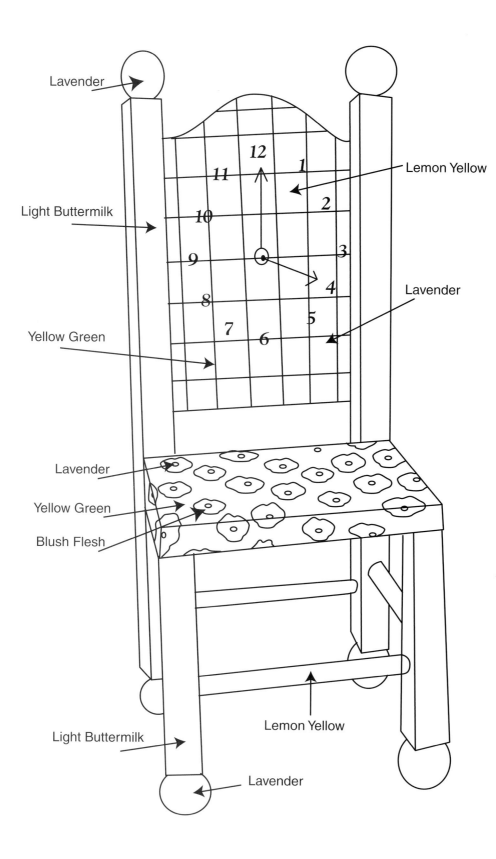

Lavender

Lemon Yellow

Light Buttermilk

Lavender

Yellow Green

Lavender

Yellow Green

Blush Flesh

Lemon Yellow

Light Buttermilk

Lavender

GINGHAM &
CHERRIES

CROSS STITCH QUILT

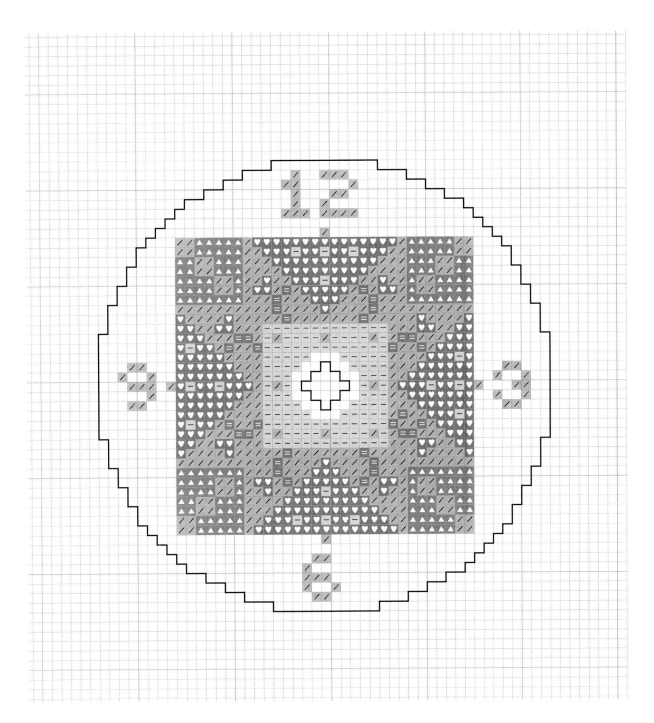

CROSS STITCH QUILT

LUMINOSITY OF TIME

ENGLISH
COTTAGE

CABIN TIME

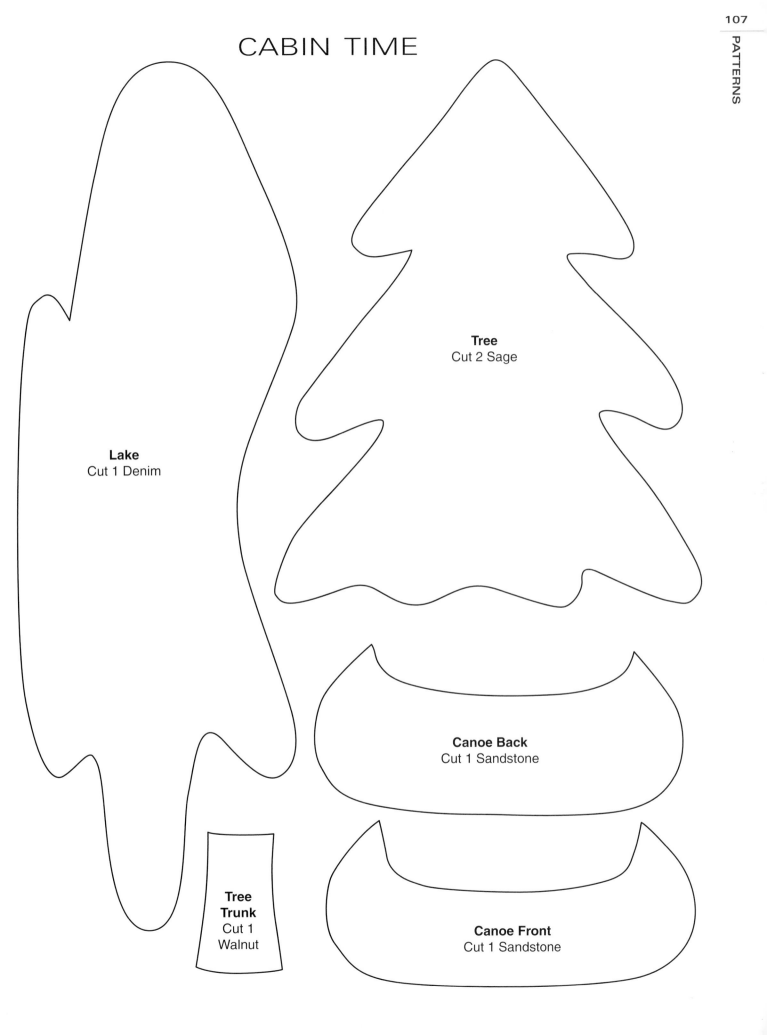

Lake
Cut 1 Denim

Tree
Cut 2 Sage

Canoe Back
Cut 1 Sandstone

Tree Trunk
Cut 1 Walnut

Canoe Front
Cut 1 Sandstone

STRAW HAT

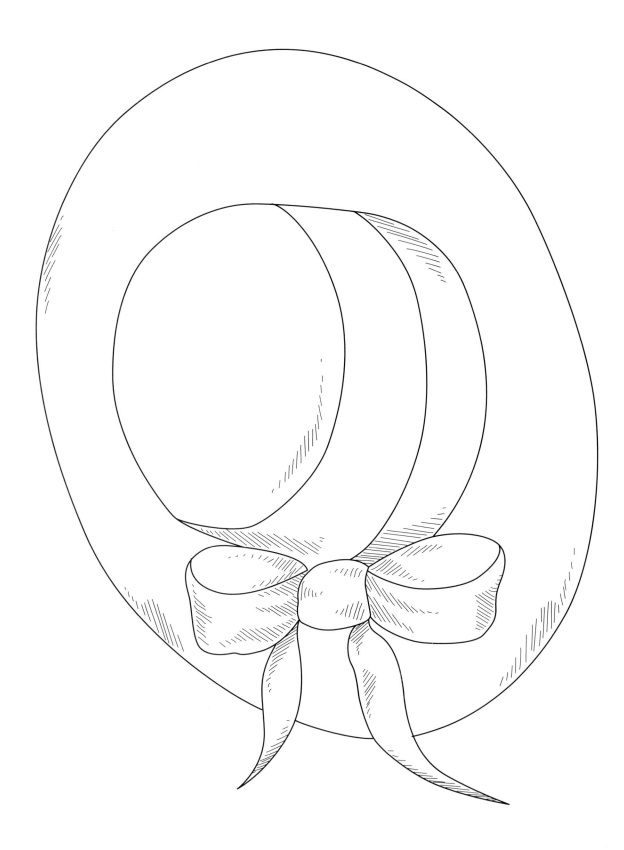

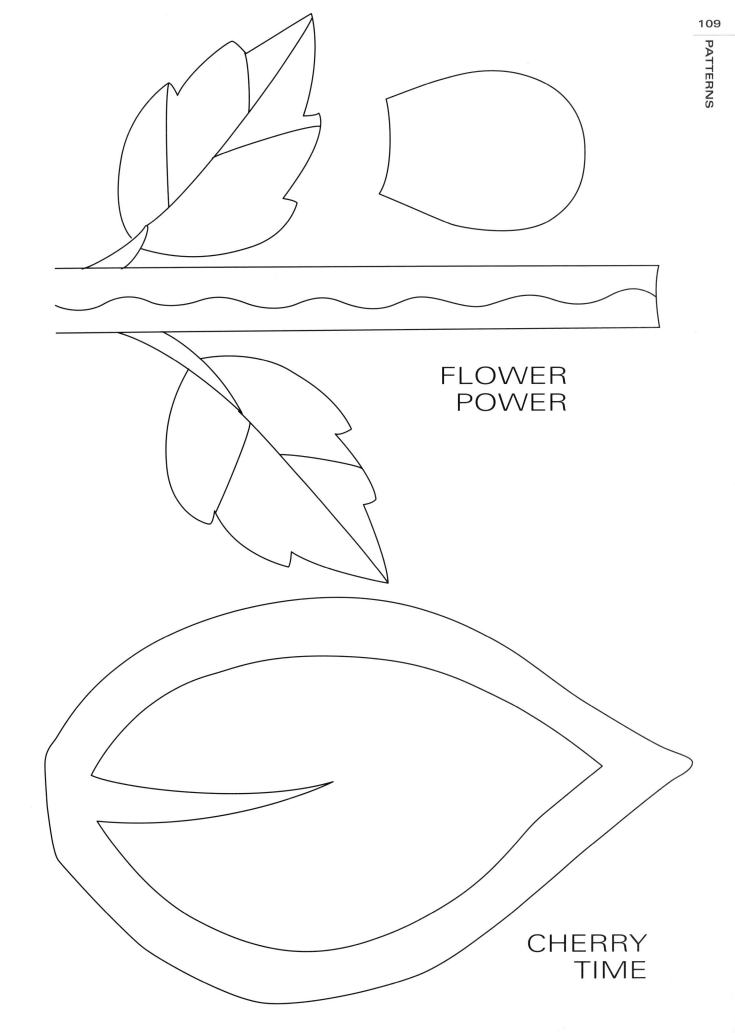

FLOWER
POWER

CHERRY
TIME

GRANDFATHER CLOCK

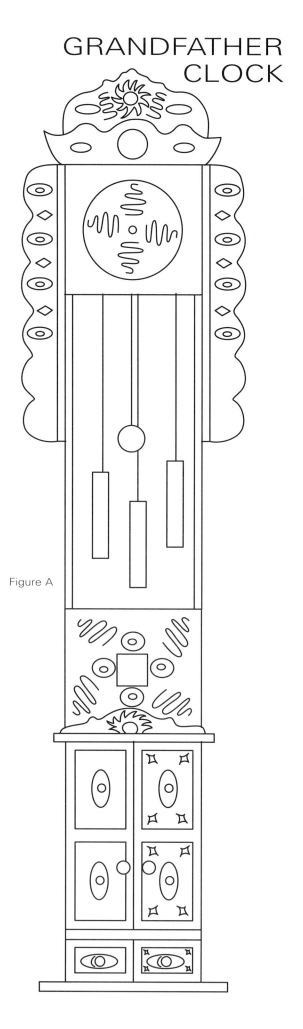

Figure A

FOLK ART BOX

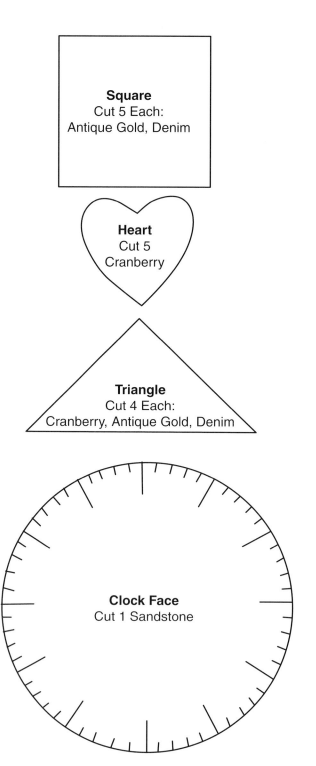

Square
Cut 5 Each:
Antique Gold, Denim

Heart
Cut 5
Cranberry

Triangle
Cut 4 Each:
Cranberry, Antique Gold, Denim

Clock Face
Cut 1 Sandstone

SAND DOLLARS

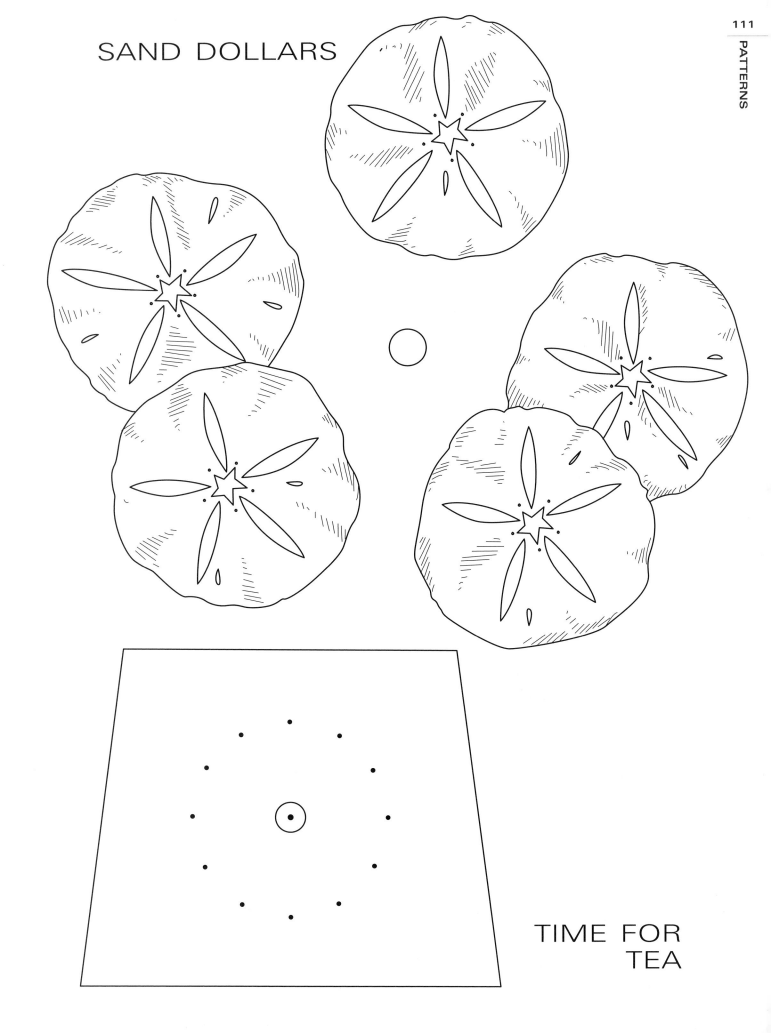

TIME FOR
TEA

Sources

Aida Cloth

Charles Craft, Inc.
(910) 844-3521
www.charlescraft.com

Beads

Elizabeth Ward and Co.
(301) 897-8311
www.bluemoonbeads.com

The Beadery
(401) 539-2432
www.thebeadery.com

Brushes/Tools

Loew-Cornell
(201) 836-7070
www.loew-cornell.com

Embroidery Floss

DMC
(973) 589-0606
www.dmc-usa.com

Felt

Kunin Felt
(603) 929-6100
www.kuninfelt.com

Glues/Adhesives

3M
(651) 737-1256
www.mmm.com

Adhesive Technologies
(603) 926-1616
www.adhesivetech.com

Beacon Adhesives
Signature Marketing
(800) 855-7283
www.beacon.com

Crafter's Pick
(800) 776-7616
www.crafterspick.com

Therm O Web
(847) 520-5200
www.thermoweb.com

Leather

The Leather Factory
(817) 496-4414
www.leatherfactory.com

Metal/Wire Mesh

AMACO
(800) 925-5195
www.amaco.com

Paint & Stain Products

Delta Technical Coatings, Inc.
(800) 423-4135
www.deltacrafts.com
(Also Glues/Adhesives, Stencils)

DecoArt
(606) 365-3193
www.decoart.com

Design Master
(303) 443-5214
www.dmcolor.com

Duncan Enterprises
(559) 291-4444
www.duncancrafts.com
(Also Glues/Adhesives)

Krylon
(216) 515-7693
www.krylon.com

MinWax
(815) 344-1343
www.minwax.com

Plaid Enterprises
(678) 291-8100
www.plaidonline.com

Paper, Punches

DMD
(501) 750-8929
www.dmdind.com

Emagination Crafts, Inc.
(866) 833-9521
www.emaginationcrafts.com

Palettes

Masterson Art Products, Inc.
(800) 965-2675
www.mastersonart.com

Pens

Sakura
(800) 776-6257
www.gellyroll.com

Polymer Clay, Tools

Kato Polyclay
Van Aken International
www.vanaken.com

Rubber Stamps

Magenta
(450) 922-5253
www.magentarubberstamps.com

Stencils

American Traditional Stencils
(603) 942-8100
www.americantraditional.com

Wire

Artistic Wire
(630) 530-7567
www.artisticwire.com

Toner
(413) 789-1300
www.tonerplastics.com

Wood Products

Walnut Hollow
(800) 950-5101
www.walnuthollow.com
(Also clock movements, hands, woodburning pen, oil pencils)

Forster
(800) 777-7942
www.diamondbrands.com